There Isn't Enough Toilet Paper in the World

The Enemy within General Motors Is General Motors

Rino Pagnucco

VANTAGE PRESS
New York

FIRST EDITION

Copyright © 1996 by Pag's Path, Inc.

Published by Vantage Press, Inc.
516 West 34th Street, New York, New York 10001

Manufactured in the United States of America
ISBN: 0-533-11789-5

Library of Congress Catalog Card No.: 96-90029

0 9 8 7 6 5 4 3 2

This book is dedicated to my writing partner and best friend who never got to see our project completed.

This book is dedicated to all the real working Americans who go to work every Monday morning or afternoon or midnight shift. It is especially dedicated to all the front- or first-line supervisors, no matter what business they are in. To all the real working Americans who have lost their jobs but somehow continued on. To all the real working Americans who work overtime or more than one job so life can be better for others. To all the small businessmen and -women who have dedicated their lives to putting other people to work and making their lives a better way of living. To all the real working Americans who help get milk on the table, bread in the toaster, and that roast in the oven. To all the real working Americans who protect our neighborhoods and country. To all of the above who have since passed on so that we could have better lives. To executives and politicians who believe we cannot give up our jobs for cheap foreign labor. We have the best talent in Americans to get the job done.

We are dedicated to seeing that all the executives and politicians who have only thought of themselves while lining their own pockets become the next unemployed!

Contents

Foreword

This book, which we hope you are about to read and we sincerely hope you will enjoy, is the work of two GM employees with combined experience of over half a century. What we want to do is try to help you, the reader, understand what really goes on in an assembly plant. Please keep in mind that we are only relating instances from our own experiences at GM plants. The names and locations of these plants are relatively unimportant to you, regardless of how important or vivid they were to us. We may, from time to time, mention one site or another, but the thought you need to be aware of is that the site makes little difference to the outcome. We may mention someone by name, but the intent is to only do this when it can be construed positively. When the negative is the case, we will try to use either the position title, such as general foreman, superintendent, manager, or director, or, in the extreme, a fictitious name. Many people may think they recognize themselves when, in fact, we probably forgot all about them and were actually referring to someone else. But when things are as difficult as they were, and still are, it's easy to do that.

We feel that if someone is upset, perhaps it will inspire him to change for the betterment of General Motors. That's the whole point as far as we are concerned. By and large, we have enjoyed working for General Motors. After all, they paid the bills and helped us live a fairly good life. The point is to try to make someone see that things haven't changed from as bad as they were then to now. Who knows? Maybe someone will read this, see himself or someone he knows, and maybe, just maybe, he will change. We are not talking about the workers on the floor. We are talking about the superintendents, plant managers, and executives who, for some mysterious reason, always think it's the people or workers under them who need to change, not themselves.

As you read through this book you might tell yourself it is five to ten years too late. That was then, things have changed, and that type of environment and behavior couldn't possibly exist anymore. The automotive industry, especially General Motors, wants you to believe that. But other people might say that if they didn't know any better and if we took the words *General Motors, Ford*, and *Chrysler* out of our text, we were actually talking about "their" company. They are saying this because, yes, the situations that are in this book are oh, so real and many of us either have experienced similar situations in the past or are living through them presently.

General Motors, along with other key players in the automobile industry, is probably saying, "What a bunch of crap!" They are making more money than ever and can't make enough cars and trucks to keep up with the demand. So, let's get something straight here. "They," being top management, really and truly are making more money. You see, they are still employed. They are not part of the 300,000-plus American automobile workers comprised of unemployed assembly line workers, clerks, secretaries, engineers, etc., not to mention all the workers in auto-related small businesses that went under and at the over fifty plants that have been shut down and sent to foreign countries for cheap labor and tax breaks. Why wouldn't "they" be making more money?

Our government continuously says that small business is what America is all about. Yet, in turn, the government is making it harder and harder for the American people with dreams of someday owning their own business to realize their dreams. The

Americans who presently own their business are fighting a losing battle to keep on existing. Federal and state laws and restrictions have become tougher and tougher on small businesses. And with the present direction that the automobile industry is headed in and the Clinton administration's passing of NAFTA, we are going to send our decent-paying jobs to other countries first. That means whatever other lower-paying jobs are leftover, Americans can have. Our present government says unemployment is at an all-time low and that there are more jobs than ever before. Yes, we agree, there are "more lower-paying jobs" than ever before. Some people call these jobs "McJobs." There are numerous studies that say that even though there are more jobs today, the percentage of middle-income families has decreased so much that our society will soon consist of two class structures: RICH, which can be viewed as "top management," and POOR, which can be viewed as the "worker."

We, as tax-paying American citizens, are being deceived by top management and political professionals, and we have to help each other become more aware of what is going on around us. We have to become more aware of our purchasing power. We have an obligation to our ancestors, ourselves, our children, and our country to go in the right direction. We want other countries to look at America as a country of prosperity and greatness and Americans as caring and giving, not as easy marks. We hope this book brings awareness to everyone that the automobile industry is what makes our economy move in various directions. To let other countries build our cars and take our jobs while America experiences an increase every year of homeless people, skyrocketing welfare, and crime and deficit problems means we are truly out of control. There isn't enough toilet paper in the world to clean this mess up unless Americans focus on making America number one!

We will never stop saying, "BE AMERICAN, BUY AMERICAN, and make sure it's from an American-owned company built IN AMERICA."

Acknowledgments

I would like to take this opportunity to thank all the people who have helped and given me the support to go ahead with something that I strongly believe in: my partner, who has trusted me to go on with the business of publishing our book, and my family, who never once thought I was "NUTS" (WELL, MAYBE ONCE) but encouraged me to follow all my dreams.

Thank you to all the "working-class people" that I have come into contact with over the past thirty-plus years, starting with my first job delivering newspapers at the ripe old age of eleven to my present retirement in 1994 from General Motors, who made this book possible.

Thank you to all the clubs and organizations that I have been involved with since I was a kid. The Boy Scouts of America, the Jaycees of America, and the Rotary helped me learn to treat people like I want to be treated and how to help people that can't help themselves. I have met many terrific people in my travels and have learned that no matter what you do in your lifetime, it's about people and whether it's a hobby or an organization or your profession, you should always strive to be the best you can be.

Thank you to Local 1219 out of Lima, Ohio, for putting a sign on Interstate I-75 that reads: "BUY AMERICAN. The Job You Save May Be Your Own." I also want to thank an unknown person in Michigan who in 1990 had a sign on the back of his car that read: "This is your country too! Help take care of it. Do your job well & buy American Products." God bless you, whoever you are.

Thank you to my heroes. I have always been a big supporter and am very grateful to the Vietnam vets and all veterans of foreign wars. I want to extend my deepest sympathy to all the families of my deceased close friends who passed away at very early ages without fulfilling the working person's dream of a full life and a happy retirement.

Thank you to my kids, Greg and Lesley, for just being there when I needed them.

Thank you to my wife, Marie, who has stood by me, encouraged me, and always supported my efforts to start, continue, and finish this project.

THANK YOU ALL

Rino Pagnucco

1

The Beginning

by Rino Pagnucco

"How far would you have to go back in time to recall when they used to build real cars? Remember the 1956 Oldsmobile? You could build five cars today with all the steel and chrome used in that one car." I think we have all met someone or known someone—someone older, of course—who has said something similar to this statement. OK, OK, maybe it was a 1955 Buick Special, a 1955 Chrysler Desoto, or a 1957 Lincoln. The point is, What we have lost in today's vehicles is the high standard of engineering and the high quality of assembly that went into these prehistoric, wonderful machines. Have you heard of anyone re- storing a 1991 Chevrolet Caprice, a 1989 Escort, or a 1987 Dodge Aires? I don't think so.

The designs today make cars resemble jelly beans with wheels. My brother, who is a wood model maker by trade, told me that the reason we are seeing cars that have a lot more curves in them is because it's harder to see the design flaws. If the hood, fenders, and doors don't fit properly, you can't see it as easily with the human eye. If the fin of a 1957 Chevy or a 1957 Ford Thunderbird was off by one-thousandth of an inch, you could see it a block away. This was due to all the angles in those older cars compared to the cars of today, which are basically round.

1

My father, an Italian emigrant and a finish carpenter by trade, was by far the smartest man I have ever known. He used to build homes, custom-built homes, just like those old cars. They stood strong and beautiful. Long ago he told me times were changing so much and so fast and that people were not building quality homes anymore. They just wanted to build more of them, all the same size and in less time. He just couldn't do that anymore. He said, "I would rather not build any homes than to continue building them in this manner." I have to think back now and wonder whether, without realizing it back then, this was the beginning of the end. He also told me that the really sad part about this whole situation was that this kind of behavior was now acceptable. It is OK to receive anything, even something as important as your home, knowing it was not constructed to the specifications stated on the blueprint.

I remember the first full-time job I had, at the ripe old age of eighteen, after graduating from high school. It was at Oakwood Hospital in Dearborn, Michigan. Even there in a hospital I could see, but at the time did not realize, the importance of quality. I used to think the head dietitian was crazy. She went about checking on everything, sampling the food, making sure all the food trays were set up right, ensuring that the patients on salt-free diets didn't have salt and the diebetics didn't have sugar, and so on. You could kind of call her the chief inspector. I kept saying to myself that the people we were serving were sick and who cared whether the knives and forks were on the left side of the tray or the right side of the tray? To her it mattered and it did make a difference, not only to the integrity of the hospital, but also to the patients who were in the hospital.

I didn't really know how important quality was at the time even though it was being taught all around me. I knew I liked receiving it, but I wasn't sure if I was giving it out. Now that I have thirty years of experience, I feel the need to tell everyone, especially General Motors, the American automobile industry, and the American public, where we are and what we have to do to stop the deterioration of quality and pride in America, which, in my eyes, if it continues, would lead to sending more of our products and jobs to foreign countries.

2

We Hire In

by Les Wheeler

To some of you reading this, it may seem like ancient history, but we both hired into Detroit Diesel in April 1964. As I am writing this, more than thirty years later, we remember a time when we could look someone straight in the eye and tell him, "Hell, I ain't even that old," when he told us that he had a certain number of years in. It seemed pretty funny then, because, I guess, we never thought that we would ever stay in any place that long.

I remember the circumstances of my hiring very well. I was up at the pool hall, that den of iniquity. As my mother used to so often tell me, "You'll come to no good hanging around that place." Of course, she neglected to tell me, at the time, that my own dad and all of his brothers (four) and my grandfather had spent a great deal of their time in the same den. That was, I'm sure, different in her eyes, and I'm equally sure that some of those who hung around the pool hall eventually did come to no good. I, myself, know a few. Where they are now is beyond me.

Anyway, there I was sitting in the pool hall and a friend of mine, Jerry (a fictitious name), came up and asked me, "Do you have your car here?" I told him I did, it was parked in the back, why did he want to know? He showed me a help-wanted ad from one of the Detroit papers for a number of job titles. I must confess that I had no idea what most of them were or what skills were needed to perform any of them. I did notice that some were for inspectors: bench and line. I felt pretty sure that I could inspect benches and lines, although I had no idea why anyone would want to. Keep in mind that I had a job; I worked in the pool hall for $1.25 per hour and all the extra money I could hustle. I was attending a local community college at the time, and this job paid for tuition, books, and dating and kept gas in the car. I had no real need for another job, especially one in a factory. The last thing I think I wanted to be when I grew up was what was commonly known as a "shop rat." At the time, I had no idea what that was either, but I had heard that it wasn't good. I later found out that wasn't necessarily true.

Getting back to the real story here, Jerry wanted me to take him up to the GM Detroit Diesel plant so he could apply for some of the job openings. It is mostly owned by Roger Penske now. Under Penske's leadership it has recaptured the market share lost by running it the GM way. I have found out in our many years in this business that higher management tells everyone in the world how they are going to run the business, but in many, many cases they are really only mouthing the words. There are some isolated instances where plants or staffs do operate that way, but it's usually only until someone finds out they are. That someone I refer to is downtown at the sacred palace known to outsiders as the GM Building. At the time, I didn't even know where the place was located; yet in later years I would know every nook and cranny of that place and most of the people within. You see, my partner Rino's last two years of his career were spent working there. He worked or should I say his traveling orders came from the seventh floor. He was a GM corporate dealer auditor. Now, if you can't believe a dreaded auditor, who else are you going to believe? One of the signs on the seventh floor of the General Motors Building states: "In God We Trust and Everyone Else We Audit!'' That's important to know, because this is really a story about people, not a place. When I left Detroit Diesel in 1976, I found that you really don't miss the place; you only miss the people in the place.

Jerry tried to tell me where the plant was, but I couldn't place it until I realized that it was the plant I could see across the street from about the sixteenth green at the Rouge Golf Course, as it was known in those days. With this information, Jerry and I proceeded to head for the plant. He had high hopes of getting a good job, and I was just killing time until I started work at the pool hall later. It was early March and still kind of chilly in the morning, so when we arrived at the plant, Jerry suggested that I come in and wait for him instead of sitting in the car. Now that didn't sound like too bad of an idea at the time, as I had no idea that it would lead to my spending over a quarter of a century working for General Motors.

I went in with Jerry and thought I would just take a seat, read the morning *Free Press*, and work the crossword puzzle until Jerry had finished whatever it is they make you do when you apply for a "real" job. It was not that I had never had a real job before, as I had worked for a small tool and die shop for the summer after I had graduated from high school. Perhaps one of the worst jobs I ever had before that was working six months for my dad. Boy, that taught me never to work for a relative! Thankfully, he let me quit to take the summer job.

Unbeknownst to me, sitting and reading the newspaper was not in my cards for that day and for many, many other days to follow. The head of the personnel department's name was Eric (a fictitious name). Just as I was settling in to read the newspaper, good old Eric came up, jabbed a sheaf of papers in my face, and shouted, in what was probably his best gruff voice, "Fill these out!" Well, let me tell you, I was only eighteen at the time and I knew the voice of authority when I heard it. In my mind, I suppose I said, "Yes, Dad," and started to fill out the forms. I figured this would be a great waste of their time and mine, as I was still sure I had no marketable skills in a plant the size of this one. The small shop I had been employed at had only one to two hundred employees on the rolls at any one time. So size alone made Detroit Diesel seem like a whole new universe to me. But reacting as I was to Eric's gruffness and "take charge" attitude, I filled them all out. I would still swear to this day that part of the overall hiring process was based on how fast you finished the forms.

I got caught up in my own little world, and I never really noticed that Jerry was still filling out the first page as I went on to the next steps. By the time the whole process was over for me, he was still filling out forms. Of course, it could have been that even though I fooled around more than most in high school, I did find the time to pay attention now and then, which is more than I could say for Jerry. Not to put the knock on my pal Jer, because he taught me how to remove a carburetor from any engine in under three minutes by the light of the moon or a nearby streetlight and when to use top or bottom right-hand English when playing snooker for more money than you had on you. You know, neat things that you wouldn't pick up in a Catholic high school or your local community college. Sorry to say, but Jerry never got a job at Diesel. He didn't have a high school education, as he had dropped out in his last year to help out around the house with some extra money after his dad left for parts unknown. I don't know whether not getting the job was good or bad for Jerry, as I hardly ever saw him again after I took the job.

I had filled out forms, taken a physical, filled out some more forms, and was beginning to think that there was an end to all of this when Eric came up and ordered me into a small office. Sitting in the office was a tall white-haired man who looked to be in his early fifties. I was to find out later that he was actually in his early sixties. He had the same "pleasant" manner that Eric had as he told me to sit down at the small desk in the small

7

office. Not being particularly stupid, even at that young age, I did as I was told. He opened what I surmised to be a blueprint of a small shaft of some sort. I had taken two years of drafting in high school and one full semester in college and had so noted on my application forms. Eric was, or must have been as smart as he was gruff, as he had noticed this and saved me from life on the assembly line. Obviously, if I was smart enough to pass these classes in school, there was that slim chance that I could become an "inspector." Which, at the time, to me, was as foreign a job as any other in the plant. Gill (a fictitious name) was the foreman in the inspection area, and he and Eric had a deal going. For every good candidate Eric recommended to Gill first, he would get a cup of coffee from Gill. If I was to, wonder of wonders, "work out" to Gill's satisfaction, he would receive another. I was to find out about this little "deal" they had had going for years and then cut my own deal with Eric. Only by then the price had gone up to two cups of coffee. The price of a favor was very frequently based on coffee. The power of one cup for free could cut a lot of red tape and make good things happen where bad was the norm for others. There is probably some deep psychological story behind this coffee ritual that still exists to this day and probably will until all the GM plants are closed and only the Japanese transplants exist.

Gill pointed to a few simple details on the print and asked me simple questions about the shaft and inspection tools in general. The whole event couldn't have taken over ten minutes. But unbeknownst to me, my whole life was going to change drastically and dramatically forever. Two marriages, two sons, and over thirty years later, it still goes on.

Believe it or not, Rino went through basically the same process one month later. The main character was still Eric, but in Rino's case, the supervisor doing the intereviewing was different. We would find out how much different years later. His name was Tocco (a fictitious name) and he was Italian. It kind of reminded

Rino of his father; they had something in common. They both came from Italy and both spoke broken English. Unbeknownst to Rino, they both knew each other. Rino admired and respected both these men. Gradually, Rino began to feel that he had passed some test and might be in line for a position at the plant. Not sure enough to give notice to the hospital he was working at, but enough to at least keep an open mind on the subject should it ever come up again.

At the time, Rino was working as a cook's helper at Oakwood Hospital and was seriously thinking of pursuing a career in the field of food. Strangely enough, as I look at him now, he has realized his goal. Only catch is that it's in food processing, as in the intake of lots of it. Let's just say that he hasn't missed a lot of meals lately. Before he gets his two cents in, I haven't either. The best way to tell us apart is that he's the tall one. I'm a legend in my own mind, but you can't tell that by looking at us.

The hiring process was the same, but the next sequence of events was decidedly different. I was in my driveway working on my car when this guy pulled in and got out of the car. Now in my neighborhood, which was on the west side of Detroit, in 1964, when some unknown dude pulled into your driveway it usually didn't mean good news was going to befall you. I casually reached under the hood and grasped the largest wrench available to me. In those days, you might say I had a few less than friendly friends and wasn't taking any chances. He approached my car and asked me my name. I asked just why did he want to know? He replied that he had a telegram to deliver. I laid down the wrench and walked over to him as I said, "Aw fuck, I've been drafted!" And that, folks, is exactly what I thought. After all, the war in Vietnam was going on and I had taken a physical just a few months earlier, so the thought was sincere and from the heart. I told the deliveryman to hit the road; I wasn't going to tip anyone for bringing my draft notice. Later, I would feel bad about that, as he didn't know what the telegram was and even if he did, he hadn't sent it. However, I did not feel bad enough to try to find out who he was and send him a tip either.

When I opened the telegram and found out that I wasn't drafted but had a job to report to the next day, I was surprised, to say the least. I was not so surprised that I didn't report to work the next day. I did suffer some pain that night, though, because the telegram said to report to work as a "bench and line" inspector. I still had no idea as to why anyone would want to inspect benches and lines, but I vowed to dedicate myself to the task so I could save up enough money to attend college full-time in the fall. That's right, boys and girls, I hired in for the summer of '64 and stayed on for the duration. They were going to pay me the outrageous sum of $3.33 per hour and time and a half for overtime and Saturdays, plus double time for Sundays! About this time, I don't think I cared what I had to do to the benches and lines, but I was ready for it. My only problem was, How does one dress to inspect benches and lines?

Not having any way to find out, I sort of semisolved the problem by dressing casually nice. That means that I dressed like I was going to play golf at a country club: nice slacks, but not my best, and a golf shirt that was light-colored, in case it was a white-collar job these bench and line inspectors did. I was soon to find out that I had dressed "up" for the job and that bench and line inspectors meant "where" we worked, not what we inspected. Imagine my distress! It could have been worse; I could have worn a white shirt and a tie and been laughed off the job before I had even grown to hate it.

I remained a bench and line inspector for three years. I did progress through the ranks of the classification, lest some of you think I was just a shop rat who got lucky. I became a group leader or utility man after two years and then had my own department to inspect in and for. Years later—as a matter of fact, to this day—I still say that was the best job I've ever had and that I should have kept it instead of taking promotions, but I really wanted to

10

be in charge and to run things my way. I wanted to get things done fast, right, and better than the time before, and I thought I could get other people to follow me rather than me following them. I was right about that, I could get people to follow me, and sometimes I was so good at it that they thought they were leading the train, not riding in it.

I left that job to go on salary in February 1968 as a junior methods engineer. It was a new department and offered me the chance to really get into the mainstream and show what I could do without the restraints that the union places on the hourly employee that wants to get ahead. (Remember, this was in 1968.) The department was supposed to monitor all assembly methods and to determine the best ones. If none existed, we were to write one and get the foremen and workers in the area to agree to it and then use it. Sounds simple, but in reality it didn't really work too well, as we had no authority to enforce the use of anything we came up with. Eventually, we became auditors of the methods that they were using and only wrote or changed the method when there was a problem. This also was a problem, as too often we were viewed as the bad guys who caused trouble whenever we showed up—a sign of the future and how change was going to be dealt with.

Regardless whether the change was going to help or not, any change was going to be perceived as bad, because that's the way it had always been and that's the way it ought to stay. Even in the face of obvious advantages to the organization and the individuals, change was not the way things were going to be. To this day, I have a downright almost violent reaction when someone tells me we are doing something, right or wrong, "because that's the way we've always done it." Nothing will stand in the way of progress more than that statement, other than perhaps: "That can't be done." Now that statement only means one of two things to us: you personally can't do it or you don't want to try to do it. It can be done if someone wants it to happen. We've

11

done some really serious shit that managers, other supervisors, and some very lazy people have emphatically stated, in no uncertain terms, couldn't be done. You don't know if it's going to be good or bad sometimes until you try it. Remember your dad always saying, "If you never try, you'll never know"?

Rino—remember Rino?—received his telegram from Detroit Diesel to report to work while he was on his honeymoon. When they returned from the trip, he was sorting through the mail and found a telegram. He made the same assumption I did when I received mine, which was to think he had been drafted. Obviously, he was wrong, too. He finally opened it and, much to his surprise and delight, found out that he was to report to work the following day at 7:00 A.M. The problem was that he had to quit his job at the hospital on some pretty short notice, like a phone call in the night to tell them he wouldn't be in on Monday. For that matter, he wouldn't be in on Tuesday or any other day from here on out. Needless to say, the staff at the hospital cafeteria was less than thrilled with the news. To this day, I think they still hold it against him. I'm sure if he was to be involved in an accident right in front of Oakwood Hospital, he would tell the driver of the ambulance to take him anywhere else just on the outside chance that they would recognize the name during admitting and perform a lobotomy during his stay. Farfetched, I know, but when you come from our backgrounds in Detroit, nothing is too farfetched to be too cautious.

Unluckily, Rino forgot to set the alarm and was almost late for his first day of work. He has told me this story quite often over the years, and I've always believed that my version of the actual "truth" is as I've imagined. I think, Here's a guy just back from his honeymoon and he set the alarm, but he also thought he had time for a little hanky panky and just miscalculated on the amount of time he had to get prepared before he had to go.

One thing you have to understand is that in 1964 it was tough to find a job. Any job, let alone a good job that paid more

12

than minimum wage. Tough to find and tough to keep. Believe us when we say that management knew this and took full advantage of that fact. From the beginning, you were lied to. You were told lies such as that you were not entitled to any union representation until you had reached that milestone of ninety days of seniority. In reality, that meant that you didn't want to be late for work even once, and I'm not talking hours here; I'm talking minutes. God forbid if you missed a day for whatever reason. You really had to pray that no close friends or relatives died during this probationary period. That may sound foolish to you, but try to remember that in 1964 it wasn't. We both knew of people discharged for lesser offenses than that. The supervisor rationalized it out to himself that maybe your family was prone to dying and this could turn into a regular thing. As if his family wasn't prone to the same problem. They just had the decency not to die during the nonemployee period in his life. Is it any real wonder that when people did make their ninety days they did indeed take on some of the characteristics that were attributed to them?

Another method used is the one where supervisors would get together and talk about someone who could hear them talking, to brag about what they were going to do to him. Comments like: ''I'll fire his ass''; ''He'll wish he had never hired into this area''; and: ''He'll be sorry he ever called the union on me!'' were not uncommon. In truth, they were all too commonly stated and all too often carried out. Earlier, we implicated the union in this process because, in actuality, you were entitled to union representation at the end of thirty (not ninety) days in any case of alleged discipline. The union had no problem taking your money in dues as soon as you hired in, but like management, they didn't want any ''troublemakers'' either. Someone that was prone to having people in their family die might lead to other problems later, and that might not be good for the union or management. We doubt if they actually stated it in those terms, and perhaps they didn't even visualize what they were doing until it was too late for them, too. One thing about the union is that if the members were upset with their leadership, they could at least be voted out of office. This is an interesting concept that never really caught on in the management ranks. Not unsurprisingly. We saw a lot of changes in the union due to the phenomenon of voting for leadership. If you didn't provide it, you were fairly well assured of relearning the job you had before someone became upset with the guys before you. Don't get us wrong here. We are not in any way knocking the union. It was the problem we were to face a hundred times over during the years, poor leadership, not the goals or the jobs, but the means. The means do not justify the end. The end has to be stated clearly, and then everyone has to work towards that end. That end cannot be the protection of someone's personal power base, which may put the organization at risk in the future. That's just the way things were, and we hope you can see why the need for change becomes so self-evident. The need to change a system that is running headlong into disaster. This is a system that spawned the most radical union leaders and members that we have ever seen. Later, we will focus on some of the results of this strategy. We use the term *strategy* very loosely here, as that would almost imply that there was a plan and that would be giving credit where none is due.

Well, back to Rino. He hired into an assembly department under a fellow Italian supervisor. As I referred to earlier, Rino was almost late on his first day. Good thing he wasn't, as there would be no story from his point of view if he had been late. Let me clarify the statement "almost late." When one starts at seven o'clock in the morning, almost late is 6:58 or 6:59, not when Rino showed up at 6:45 A.M. That's fifteen minutes early, not "almost late." But after your new supervisor chews on your butt for five minutes of the fifteen you are early, you get the message. Tomorrow is another day and you can bet your butt that our

14

friend Rino was ready to go at 6:30 A.M., just like all the other nonseniority employees in the area.

I've already told you that Rino was six-foot-two and 195 pounds (that was in 1964), and you should have some perspective of a fairly large individual here. I'm not a really big guy myself, five-foot-eight, 150 pounds (then, not now; I'm still that tall but weigh a touch more than I did then, if you will buy 30 pounds as a touch more), but when I shake hands with Rino, my hand gets swallowed up by his. We are talking about the proverbial pair of ham hocks here, folks. So, what's the best job to give someone of that size and stature? The one with the smallest parts! Of course, you guess it right away!

And, that's the way it was and to some degree it still is. We've seen good people on the wrong job quit before lunch or go to lunch and never return. A good job sometimes wasn't worth the physical and mental aggravation, regardless of the pay and the benefits. However, keep in mind that Rino had just quit the only job he ever had that paid more than minimum wage and besides, he was a hard worker who wouldn't let this stand in his way. He decided to do it anyway. For those of you who have a ruler handy, check this out. One of his jobs was to torque (which means to tighten) the fuel jumper lines. A little crash course in diesel engines seems to be in order here for some of you. Fuel jumper lines are little copper tubes that cross over from the fuel lines in the cylinder head to the fuel injector. There was one fuel injector and two jumper lines for each cylinder, and the average number of cylinders per engine was three. Well, when I say little, I mean little. The brass connection nut was about one-half-inch across the flats, and the torque required to stop leaks was twelve-inch pounds. Rino would overtorque these little suckers by hand and then have to loosen them to meet the specifications. Took him a while to get the hang of that. By the way, did I mention that not only were they small, but they were pretty close together, too? Probably not. The two connections on the top were about three inches apart. The two connections on the bottom, however, more than made up for the abundance of space here. The socket for the torque wrench that you received from the tool crib (this is great; use the right tool for the right job) had to be ground to half its original dimension, because there wasn't enough room to tighten one if the other was on. Now, if you think about it, that means that if you used the tool as it came, you had to take one off to tighten the other. This wouldn't have been so bad, except that the crazy inspectors wanted to have both of them on and tight. What gall! And as in the case of most predators (the inspection department, on the whole, operated as an adversary to the rest of the organization, not unlike the management and union relationship), whenever they sensed that any employee was having or could be having a bad day, they swooped down on the luckless person and double-, if not triple-checked anything he had done that day. Let me tell you, That makes for some winning friendships. If an inspector died, why tell anyone? Let's just wait and see if they noticed. Some of you may remember that I was working in the opposite end of this plant as an "inspector." By the time Rino and I met each other, you can understand that someone (Rino) might be less than helpful to the new inspection supervisor, who also happened to be slightly wacky (me).

There were many other tasks involved with this job, and rather than trying to bore you to tears (or to returning the book—perish the thought) with an explanation of each task, let's just leave it at this: Rino thought the cycle was tight, fifteen minutes per job, and that assembling his part of forty-seven engines in an eight-hour day was an awesome task. Little did he realize that he would one day be the supervisor of an assembly line that had a cycle of four minutes or 120 engines per eight-hour shift.

3

The Early Years

by Les Wheeler

In the early years of my quarter-century I was an hourly employee in the inspection department classified as a "bench and line" inspector. That meant a couple of things. We inspected many and varied engine components, from oil filter adaptors to engine oil pump covers and water pump bodies. We had two four-drawer file cabinets that were filled with blueprints and job instructions. The job instructions were, to say the least, just a little lacking in scope in their shortness. You might find yourself inspecting a basket full of some part that had several gauges, a three-foot-by-six-foot blueprint, at least seven finished surfaces, etc., and had the following job instructions: "Inspect for all dimensions," the theory being that if the instructions weren't too specific, then someone could never check them all in the time allotted and then if he missed any problem that was later found in the assembly area, you could always blame him for missing it! Kind of a neat idea when you think about it. If you told someone to look for everything and then never gave him the time to do it, you could always be assured that this would cause some errors and this would then create jobs, as someone from our group was always in the stockroom sorting parts for something someone else had missed. Sort of a self-perpetuating system designed for failure. Prevention techniques were certainly not in the vogue here.

Another neat idea that didn't come into vogue until the late sixties was the practice of establishing just how many defects constituted "poor quality." This one took us a little while to catch onto. This was the basic concept: If there was one defect, find it and fix it. If there were ten, find them and fix them. If there were between ten and one hundred, let's think this over before we do anything and check out how much it costs before we go running off to find them and fix them. If there were over one hundred but less than five hundred, the cost rule applies, but then we also add in the time to fix the problem and then we make a "decision." If the problem was over five hundred and less than infinity, we would almost always decide to "let the customer find it." That was provided, of course, that the engine would start with whatever its particular problem was. I mean, let's face it, if the damn thing wasn't going to start because of its problem, even our enlightened management knew there was little sense in shipping them.

It wasn't always like this. I worked in the machining end of the plant, and Rino worked in the assembly area. Both ends (and, of course, the middle) operated with much higher quality standards than this. If you didn't do it right the first time, you did it over until you did it right. We prided ourselves on shipping the highest-quality, most reliable, and most durable engines to our customers. Everyone in the plant was proud of our product and our reputation with the customer. Our most basic customers were truck drivers, and quite frequently you would find employees at a truck stop actually soliciting comments from drivers as to how their particular engine was performing. In later years, as the quality, reliability, and durability were eroded by the "numbers" game of quality, most of us wouldn't even admit that we worked for General Motors, let alone tell a truck driver that we worked for Detroit Diesel. Hell, if they found that out, you could get yourself hurt. If not by their words, then by their actions. Sometimes these guys could get downright violent when they found out where you worked. Like it was your fault or something.

Let's set the record straight right now. Hourly employees don't set the quality standards. They just perform to the standards set by management. If the standards are high, they do good work. If the standards are low, they bitch, piss, moan, fight, and argue to maintain higher standards but are soon overwhelmed by such comments of intelligence as: "Hey, this ain't no Swiss watch; it's a diesel engine"; or: "We don't have time to do them all right; the customer knows that"; or: "If we wanted them all right, why would we have a warranty account anyhow?" Faced with trying to maintain quality in the teeth of this, the average employee would eventually just give in and go with the new standards regardless of how low they were or how wrong he knew they were. Remember, we didn't make the rules; we just played the game.

The game was generally played with no written rules. If there are no written rules, then no one knows if he is playing the game correctly. This works out pretty good for management, because if you don't know how to play the game to the rules, you could almost always be caught doing something not according to the rules. Now this becomes even more in their favor if you think of it in this light. You play the game by yesterday's rules and that works out OK until the problem you caught or missed violated the previously mentioned "numbers" rule of quality. In that case, no other rules apply except the numbers game. This also works out really well, as no one ever knows what the hell rules are in effect at any time. Ask us if this doesn't create some serious stress for anyone trying to do his job.

Some of us found ways to cope with this ever-changing standard. We simply never dropped the old standards. That means that if the blueprint said "no gouges, nicks, or scratches" on any finished gasket surface, well, that's what it meant. If you found any of the above-noted items, you red-tagged the basket and made a note in the routing or inspection file that stated that the load was rejected for whatever defect you found. This served at least

19

two purposes. First, it let the next inspector know that you had found the problem, documented the problem, and forced the supervisor to "sign off" on the problem. This was kind of neat in its own way, as very often your supervisor had no idea whether the defect you noted was a problem or not. Sometimes, if your supervisor was trying to do a good job, too, he would even try to find out if the problem was a problem. Generally, if you knew what you were doing, it was a problem and you knew it. Otherwise, why write it up? But you also knew that someone was going to OK the parts if enough pressure was brought to bear by the departmental supervisor that needed them. The only reason to note the problem was in case someone down the line didn't change the rules for the day and didn't need the parts badly enough to use them in their current state and rejected them and sent them back for reinspection and repair. In cases like this, it didn't make any difference how many times we had used parts just like this, because that rule was not in effect at this time. The new rule was. The new rule was that that particular problem was a problem today and the guy who missed it was going to have to pay for his indiscretion of the moment. This pretty much served to keep everybody on edge all the time. The order of the day was not to do a good job, but to "CYA" (cover your ass). It has been stated that with an atmosphere like this in your organization, you spend more time doing the CYA than doing your job. CYA adds a tremendous amount of wasted time to anyone's job and adds no value to the product or service you might be performing. But it does keep everyone busy and on their toes. If we had a guess, we would venture that psychiatrists would certainly benefit from the long-term effects of the stress created by such a system.

When and why did the usually high quality standards change? What caused the change? Who benefited from the changes? These are all reasonable questions that probably deserve an answer of some sort. We're going to try to do that.

When we first hired in, the standard was high quality and higher productivity. You did a damn good job and you gave 100 percent to your job every day, not just when you felt like it or on your "good days." If someone made an honest mistake, he heard about it soon and often. If you made the same type of mistake too often, you found yourself on the outside looking in. That's the way it was and should still be. The pressure comes from trying to make as many engines as you could sell.

We saw the problems then (and now) and tried to correct them. But try as we might, we could never convince anyone in charge that the customer was unwilling to accept defective products just because he got them on time or you could promise delivery faster than your competitors regardless of the quality of the finished engine. That seems to be such a basic concept that we could never understand the premise that quick in any condition was what the truck driver wanted. Remember, this is not like your car or my car, where you need it to get you to and from work or to and from the mall. If it doesn't start every time every day, well, so what? You could always call someone else in the department or take a cab. For a truck driver, this engine's performance was his livelihood. If it didn't work, the driver didn't make any money until it did. It was the powerplant that made his business go and made him money. Now maybe you can understand why a Diesel employee wouldn't volunteer the information as to whom he worked for and where he worked to a truck driver.

The desire by management to make more than they could sell, in less space than they had, was probably the main reason for the downfall of the standards. When we first hired in, you had to have at least a high school education, and we sure don't mean just the piece of paper that says you made it through four years without getting caught murdering someone or getting busted for selling drugs to your classmates. It meant a real diploma, and you had better display the qualities that it represented,

21

such as being able to read, write, and add two and two more than once.

It was important to be able to perform what seemed like simple tasks to be able to do your job. In the machine shop end of the business, you had to be able to read and interpret the blueprints to make the parts and then inspect them. In the assembly end of the business, you had to read the "bill of material" for each engine and decide which parts were needed and where they went, what torque they needed, and many other little eccentricities of each engine, as each one coming down the line was, in essence, a custom-built job. Each customer had different requirements and expected his requirements to be met each and every time.

Then the standards for quality of the product changed, and so did the standards for being hired. Remember that both of these standards were set by management and not by the employees. Believe it or not, we were actually hiring people that couldn't write their own name, let alone read a bill of material. We were actually hiring the hard-core unemployable from Detroit and its surrounding areas. This sounds like a nice thing to do to help them out and reduce the ranks of the unemployed in the Detroit area. But, in reality, the best thing to do would have been to hire and then educate them before turning them loose in an environment that required them to do things they couldn't. Some of them really wanted to work but just plain lacked the skills required to do the job. They were the ones we felt sorry for.

The blows to their egos were harsh. In many cases we would be firing the employee before his paperwork went through the personnel system. This may sound cruel and inhumane to you right now, but when we explain the pressure and stress associated with being a first-line supervisor later on, you might see that it was inevitable for both parties. It sure wasn't fun and we don't know of too many supervisors who enjoyed the firing part of the job. The sad part about this is that some supervisors never could separate the human feelings from the business end of the job and kept some of these people on the job. Kept them on to do things they never could and eventually they got their seniority and belonged in a community where they had no credentials to be in the first place.

What was the outcome from all this? Supervisors hired more people to do the jobs than were required because now they needed extra people to do the jobs. They trained (not educated) these people to do the simplest jobs and then kept them in that prison forever. You had to. You had to do something with them, and sometimes that was the best option available to you. Granted, not a good one, but the only one. A lot of these people became sweepers and chip handlers, because it didn't take that much skill to do either of those jobs. Sometimes you never changed their classifications and eventually, as their seniority increased, they actually gained higher-paying jobs and more difficult tasks ability (on paper only) because of their time in place, not their skill levels. This wasn't a problem until there was a slowdown in the business that required everyone to have a reduction in force and you had to lay off some people. Very frequently the people you had kept to help out even though they couldn't perform the simplest task in assembly would displace other people who were better qualified but had less seniority. This was not good for the efficiency of the department or the quality of the product.

4

Some Things Just Never Change

by Les Wheeler

Some things just never change. Sometimes when you think they have, you find out just how wrong you can be. General Motors has been touting their new thinking of how important their employees are to them, and then they turned right around and laid off some seventy thousand employees. Strangely, the people who are getting laid off had very little to do with the losing of $7.1 billion in 1991. One of the questions we've always asked over the years is: Why don't any of the heads that made the decisions that led to this downfall ever roll in the aisles, too? It would seem to us that if every time a plant was closed and everybody in it laid off you had to lay off one of the board members, it might never get that bad in the first place. Perhaps if there was some accountability in the process, we wouldn't have built all the excess capacity and lost all the bucks. But what a naive idea that is. That's part of the problem (if not all of the problem). The big guys were never to blame. It was always the workers on the floor in the plants. "If only they were more dedicated, if only they would work harder, if only they would do more quality work . . ." Never mind that they were only doing what they were told to do and if you even tried to voice any dissent, you were suddenly on the outside looking in. You never got the promotions you deserved or the raises you earned. You got the shitty jobs no one else wanted or could do. It's especially interesting to note those jobs that no one else could do. You knew why you got them, but you did your best anyway and when your best was better than anyone else's best, it was written off as a coincidence or that the supervisor before you had set it up and you were just reaping the benefits. Not to mention that the last three supervisors hadn't lasted three months before they bailed out of their trip to hell and, believe us here, some departments had been handled so badly before you showed up that they were just that: hell.

The story here is change. General Motors has been saying that they have changed. We're here to tell you that some people have changed (very few and at lower levels than required to make real change happen), but then so have fashions and styles of cars. We no longer drive Bel Airs or Impalas or Citations or Vegas anymore either. But don't be fooled by the words. I've been fooled more than once. I've been foolish enough to fall for the old "it's not a program . . . it's a process" routine too often to count. They tell you that crap and even if you don't believe them, you have to at least test the system to see just how much of it they do mean. Usually it's not too much. I can remember going to one particularly interesting and seemingly informative class at GM Truck and Bus when I was still in manufacturing as a supervisor. I think the name of the class was Participative Management. It was a class where management was supposed to listen to the employees and try to work together to save the world (General Motors). I can remember thinking that this was the same stuff that got my ass in a big sling for trying to do the same thing at the old GM Detroit Diesel when I worked there in the late sixties and early seventies. Could have been the same class books. The thought was surely the same, no matter what they called it. It worked for me and Rino really well at Diesel until management found out we were actually doing what our employees suggested we do. The problem was that management felt they were losing control, and the next thing you would hear about was the tail wagging the dog, the inmates running the asylum, etc. We are here to tell you that in most cases the inmates do a better job of running the asylum.

That's another one of those things they tell you: the people closest to the job know how to do it best. That really sounds good, but in real life it doesn't really work because of this power loss thing that management has yet to come to grips with. It all deals with change, and they simply can't do it. Well, what the heck, I paid attention in the class and tried to learn more and I was really ready to go when I got back to work.

Welcome to the real world. The first person I saw when I got back to work on Monday was my illustrious leader. He came to my "office" on the floor, did not even say hello, picked up my training manual from the class, pitched it in the garbage can next to my office, and said, "Well, you won't need this shit anymore." It does not take a mental giant to figure out the message here, does it? I appreciated the course and the knowledge I gained but knew I could never get caught using any of my new-found skills. Guess how many of the rest of the supervisors in my plant looked forward to going to this class? Not too many.

Change, that's what we're talking about here, though, aren't we? "That's ancient history," you say. Maybe, maybe not. I was in a meeting in 1992 and the topic of discussion was the results from the beliefs and values survey we had just administered at GM Truck and Bus. This type of survey, no matter what you call it, is a reality check on how your organization perceives management. How well are things going, are we (management) getting the message across, are we doing the things that we tell them (the employees) that we are going to be doing, are we walking like we talk, etc. Regrettably, it turned out that they were not "walking at all like they talk"; it turned out to be mostly talk and very little walk at all. Unfortunately, they didn't like what they were hearing at all. In some cases, they disputed the data. In other cases, they denied the data. In some cases, they twisted the responses until they meant what management wanted them to say. As a prime example here, try this one on for size. In one case where "fear of reprisal" was "reputed" to be high, the chief of the area announced that a "high" score in fear of reprisal was actually good; if people were not afraid, they simply wouldn't do their jobs. Talk about your basic trust and respect for your employees. Neat, huh? But this is the way we handle "bad news": make everyone take the survey again, because the first results were too negative and that couldn't be what the participants meant. It must be in the wording of the survey. We, obviously, had structured the wording too negatively, thus leading them; that's why they answered so poorly in their judgment of us. So rewrite the survey and make the employees take it again. Now, what do you think management might say when you ask them, "What are the correct answers so I can fill this thing out right and not have to do it again? Obviously, you are not interested in how we really feel, you have an expected answer you want to hear, so why not just tell us what you want us to say and be done with it? Better yet, why don't you just fill it out for us and skip the middleman?" That would save a lot of time when you consider that each form takes an average of thirty minutes to fill out for each employee, multiplied by 2,000 employees, equals roughly 1,000 hours. You can build a lot of cars in 1,000 hours. Don't forget all the lost hours management spends trying to dispute, discredit, or otherwise deny what you see.

Believe it or not, that's not even close to the end of it. In other meetings, with many of the so-called leaders of the organization, the discussion turned to the answers to two questions from the infamous beliefs and values survey that also spoke none too highly of top management, as the organization scored low in the area of planning and instructions on how to do our jobs. Most people felt that they were not given enough time to do their job, clear instructions to do their job, or time to adequately plan to do it right the first time (what a novel thought!). During the course

27

of the discussion, it became quite evident that it was upsetting the leader (and I use the term *leader* loosely here) of the meeting. After a period of time of trying to convince everyone that this point was closely related to having a high score in fear of reprisal and not having too much luck at it, he finally remarked, "If everyone at General Motors would spend less time questioning what they were told to do and more time doing what they were told to do, General Motors would not be in the trouble they are in today." Another fine example of trust and respect for your employees here.

I think it's bad enough that someone might say this to himself, whether he means it or not, but saying it out loud in a meeting is quite unforgivable. It certainly reflects the big problem within General Motors: Top management still thinks they are not the problem or even part of it. They still think "we" are the problem. They have forgotten that it is the sole responsibility of leadership to lead. It is their responsibility to lead us to a goal, and that goal has to be quality. It can be no other, and no one else has the responsibility to do so. To continue to cast blame on the workforce can only have one outcome: General Motors will go out of business with management pointing their fingers at the unknowing, led by the uncaring, to a humiliating end. We're sorry about that, folks, but that's the way it is. We can provide excellence and expertise at ground zero but cannot set the tone or lead the way to the promised land.

Simply doing the best we can if we are doing the wrong things will result in the same outcome: a huge going-out-of-business sale to Toyota or someone else who has the right idea, say . . . like Ford or Chrysler. We are not saying it's all management's fault, but they do bear some part of the blame and, to be sure, it is a major part. Think of it like a football team made up of all stars coached by amateurs. Even if everyone plays their collective hearts out, making one great play after another, it all comes down to losing the game if the wrong plays are called, regardless of the execution of the individuals. Doing the best you can doesn't get it with the wrong game plan. That's why football teams have been known to call an audible or change the play at the line of scrimmage when the leader, or in this case the quarterback, sees something that has changed his mind. General Motors is still using the game plan from 1950. It still involves the workers checking their brains at the door, regardless of what management says it is doing. What they say they are doing versus what they are doing will continue to be different until they wake up and look in a mirror, recognizing who has the responsibility for the mess we are in.

It was bad enough to hear this individual make the remarks, but it was worse when you recognized that he was echoing what he had heard in other, higher-level meetings. He didn't make this up on his own. Such a shame that the best efforts of the best workforce in the world are being wasted by 1950s mentality. That kind of thinking didn't work in the 1950s, but there was no effective competition to prove it wrong then and, unfortunately, there is now. If we can't voluntarily change, we will be forced to change, because General Motors will no longer be there to mismanage. Leadership is not leading. They have lost control of the helm, and just like your dad twenty years ago, they won't admit to being lost and will continue to drive around in circles until they are out of gas. If your mother was in the car, she would take away his map and insist that he stop at a gas station for directions. In our case, it's plain that we are lost and people like Dr. Deming have been running alongside the car for years telling us we have to change, but all we have done is roll up the window, turn up the radio, and step on the gas to get away from our critics. They really aren't critics, no more than Rino and I are. They are people risking everything to try to fulfill the changes we say we are trying to make. I remember an old saying I heard a long time ago that seems to apply here: "When I started, I shouted because

I thought I could change them. I shout now to keep them from changing me because it is obvious that they will not change.''

One of our executives drives a Honda Goldwing motorcycle. It has been mentioned to him, on more than one occasion, that we don't make them and Honda is not an American company but a direct competitor. Believe it or not, his reply was that it is OK because his motorcycle was made in Marysville, Ohio. Now, just in case you don't work in the industry and don't quite see the problem here, let's look at a couple of nonautomotive examples of this situation. That would be identical to me working at Ford and driving a Chevrolet because it was built in this country. How about an executive at General Electric buying a Sharp brand television or the head of Kmart shopping at Wal-Mart because it was cheaper or closer to his house. We could supply you with examples like this all day, but we're pretty sure you get the idea. We know some people don't realize the consequences because too many consumers buy way too many products that aren't produced in America, and even when they are built here, the profits don't stay here! When that happens, you still end up with a net loss of American jobs. Without a strong General Motors, Ford, and Chrysler, we are in danger of being a very large third-world country. We will assemble things, but we won't be able to purchase the things we assemble. Our kids will have to go to college to work on an assembly line, and the ones that don't go to college will sell the others hamburgers for lunch and dinner at a minimum-wage job. Think about it the next time you make a purchase. Don't get caught up in the media entrapment of how much of it was built here or how much was built there. Think of it this way: Follow the money. Where does the money go? Do the profits stay here and finance more industrial capacity or do they go to some other country and increase their standard of living at the expense of ours? Think about it before you buy or make your next purchase of anything. We have already lost a lot of jobs, and our future doesn't look promising.

How can we say that some things just never change? Easy . . . they just don't. At least not within General Motors. It seems like hundreds of years ago now, even though it's only twenty or so, but the same guys who picked the guys who are running the show now did the same things or worse. How do we know? We were there. We watched it and tried to change it. It didn't work then any more than it will now.

I'm reminded of an incident that took place on what we called the "main line" at the old Detroit Diesel when General Motors ran it. I assume it was called the main line because it was the first one, having nothing to do with any "main" process or what. Anyway, someone who had probably never been out of his office noticed that something looked "different." That something was not actually any different than it had ever been (which later personal investigation revealed to be true), but this was the first time somebody of high rank noticed. No one could tell him that until it was too late to do anything but follow through with the plan. Such as it was. The problem was that the valve guides (without going into detail, they were important to the function of the engine) "appeared" to look different. What happened was this: The valve guides were suspected of having a hardness problem. They "looked" funny. Never mind that there were several sophisticated machines available to check hardness; no, they just "looked" funny to the superintendent who happened to be hanging around the area trying to "deal" one of the female subassemblers. Well, the next thing you know, all the valve guides on the line were red-tagged to hold as possible defective materials. As any good supervisor would have done, we investigated other areas that used the same parts. They also "looked" suspicious. While all this was going on, I was trying to convince my bosses that I used to work in the area that made these parts and that they had, indeed, always looked like this. It was a by-product of the heat treating process that changed the parts to become slightly discolored so they might not "look" hard enough, but they were, in

31

fact, certified to be more than hard enough for use in the engine by the metallurgical standards lab. However, this didn't mean anything to this particular superintendent. He liked Rino, having hired him, but he didn't have a lot of use for some of us who were too young and wet behind the ears, in his opinion, to know much of anything, let alone whether the subject parts were hard enough or not. Never mind that I had personally inspected more of them than he had ever seen; that was not as important as the fact that I wasn't one of his "guys." This was doubly so as I was from the dreaded inspection department and he was from production, and heaven forbid that we should ever work together for the common good of the organization. If you think that the union and management have an antagonistic relationship, try production and inspection departments in the old days!

Well, sooner or later, it had to come down to orders. I was just following orders, and that makes it OK to do anything as wrong as you want to, especially if you have it in writing. So, we ended up having to stop all the assembly lines and send everyone home for at least the day, possibly more, as we tried to sort this out. I had the unenviable job of telling all the inspectors that they weren't going anywhere but to work. It was their job to stop shipment on all engines with the suspected parts in them, and we had to start red-tagging every engine and every part anywhere in the plant that didn't "look" good. So, off we set out to do our appointed chore and tag the suspected bad guys for future workers to find and fix. I don't know what they expected to find when they decided to do this, but it probably wasn't the amount of engines that we tagged on the line, in the test rooms, and on the shipping dock. Based on the numbers, we weren't going to ship anything for days, if not weeks, as we sorted this out and then repaired the bad-"looking" parts. Someone on top must have noticed how much money this was costing, as nothing was going out the doors to the customers. Someone had to tell the superintendent to get in his office and stay there! Remember that as all this was going on, we had been trying to convince everyone concerned that there was nothing wrong with any of the parts and we had no reason to tag or hold the engines. Higher management realized this and to save some face at this time, even if they got a piece of the superintendent's ass later, they came up with a plan. So, here's the plan: Every red-tagged engine that had the parts assembled to the head was now miraculously cured. In other words, if they were lying there in the basket, they were no good. If the same parts were on an engine, they were OK to use. Given all the facts, there is really only one conclusion now, as there was then. It was about money. Pure and simple money. It would cost too much to fix the parts; therefore, they had to be good. But, to save a little face, they had to send back all the nonassembled valve guides to be repaired. This is regardless of the fact that they had been told that the parts could not be repaired and they would have to be scrapped or used. We found out later that there was never any intention to scrap them. They were going to hold them in another building for a reasonable period and then filter them back into the assembly area a few thousand at a time. So, we really only lost a few hours' production, solidified the antagonistic relationship between two departments, and guaranteed that most people would never speak up for what was right. As a by-product of the whole mess, I went on afternoons for three months, as sort of a punishment for speaking out too candidly in time of crisis. I think the direct quote when I was informed of the plan was: "Who is the asshole that thought this one up?" Fortunately or unfortunately, as the case may be, the "who" in question happened to be standing behind me when I made that remark. Had I only known, I would have made it anyway. That's one thing I could always say: "You can put me on nights and you can try to fire me, but it will never be for not telling the truth." I still had to shave every day, and as long as I needed a mirror to shave, that's the way it was going to be.

5

Paradigms

by Les Wheeler

The word *paradigm* simply means "a rule or state that currently exists." If it's the one you believe in, it's the right one and sometimes it's the only one. Sometimes it's to the exclusion of any real sanity or reason or, worse yet, logic to the situation. Often that's all we would bring to General Motors, a little reason, sanity, or logic, and that was just too much for some people to bear. If you didn't agree with their perspective, you were obviously not a team player and you were often branded as being "negative." Many times as we write this, we look at each other and remark that to the outsider this must seem like insanity, and it is. We wish we could say *was*, but *is* is the right choice of words here. It is still going on today and has barely abated, let alone gone away.

It's too bad, but sometimes the truth still applies and hurts. As in telling the truth, which hardly ever applies and too often still hurts. The old axiom about killing the messenger didn't originate in ancient Greek mythology; it actually got its start in the boardroom of General Motors and quickly carried out to everywhere else in the organization. It was especially effective where we lived and worked in an assembly plant. If you're from this planet, and we assume most of you are, you must have heard of or you must have read at least one article referring to the "Japanese style of management," where teamwork is encouraged and rewarded. Such plants must be strange places, where workers of all levels are made to feel that their opinion means something and is valued by all.

Well, let us be among the first to tell you that this management style was invented here; we just don't use it as much as we should and, in fact, sometimes we discourage it. The only time that anyone pretends that this style is the way to go is when he is trying to use it against you. He talks of a new way of life and: "Don't check your brains at the door; we value each and every one of your ideas." Translated, this means "your ideas are good as long as they agree with ours and don't require us to change in any way at all. Then and only then are they OK. If your ideas don't require change and if your ideas don't mean that we lose any power and if your ideas don't mean that we have to sacrifice any of our position to help the organization, then your ideas are OK. After all, this isn't about making General Motors better, because they're so big that nothing could ever happen to General Motors. This is about me and my piece of the pie, because I can only see my little world."

How do you make a system like this work for any length of time? Easy, if you're in charge. Participative management has nothing to do with anything, as bad news never flows uphill. I can remember being naive enough once to believe that management wanted to know how to improve the system and, yes, that they needed to know to help make things change for the better. One of the big shots at the plant we worked in singled me out after a meeting and asked me how things were going. I asked him if he really wanted to know, and he said, "Yes, I do." Not really believing him, I asked him again if he really wanted to know and if he did, why didn't he ask the guys between him and me? There were about four layers of management between us at the time. He assured me that he didn't always get the straight scoop from them and often asked floor supervisors for their input. Being fairly young and consequently fairly dumb, I kind of half believed him. I guess I figured that what the heck could he do to me for telling him the truth? Dumb question and an even dumber answer. I proceeded to tell him just how screwed up things really were.

We were at a medical conference in the plant that had been organized at the request of the plant floor supervisors. We were having some ''slight'' problems dealing with the sudden explosion of drug use and abuse by the workforce (and sometimes the supervisors themselves), and we were looking to the medical and the labor relations departments for help in identifying symptoms of drug use and abuse. Unfortunately, we were told in the meeting that the plant had no drug problem and to their knowledge (the medical and labor relations departments') no major drug dealers were to be found. Again, unfortunately, they were so far off the mark that it was pathetic. Reasonable estimates by those of us who knew the difference between a drug dealer and your local shoe salesman put the count at one major dealer in each building per shift and at least one major dealer on the midnight shift, as there simply weren't enough employees on midnights to support more than one dealer comfortably. This was among some of the things I related to the boss. Bad news for me. It turned out that the good doctor and the head of the labor relations department were both personal friends of the boss. If I had only known. Let's face it, if I had known I would have still told the boss. A lot of guys would say that they never knew what they had said or who they had said it to that got them into trouble and if they had only known, they would have never said it. I felt sorry for them. I knew what I said and I knew who I said it to and I was glad I said it! How else were we ever going to get any changes! Certainly not by ignoring the problems or by pretending that they didn't exist. I was rewarded for my honesty by immediately being ''allowed'' to set up my new shop in the engine test room on the second shift. (Second shift started at 4:00 P.M. and ran until 12:30 A.M., if there was no overtime, which might run it until 1:00 or 2:00 A.M.) A really handy place to work for any single guy. The bars closed before you got there, and the only dates you could set up were for breakfast or lunch with some other person on the second shift. Lucky me.

Also lucky for me was that I had a medical restriction to avoid working in excessive-noise areas (like Engine Test), and I did make note of this when informed of my new assignment. My boss told me not to worry, that I wouldn't have to go in there too often anyway and that restrictions like mine were only for hourly employees who had to work in there full-time. Strange, but the medical department knew I was a salaried employee when they advised me of the restrictions and gave it to me because I had been working in the test area for too long already. But I was already in enough trouble for telling the truth once too often, so the best thing to do was to take my medicine like a man and forget about it. However, I did have one more card to play, and since it was a high trump card, I said, "What the hell, go for it."

It was GM policy that any supervisor was required to make 125 percent over the employees under him. That sounds good, but it really means that you should make at least 25 percent more than the people you were to supervise. In my case, that was pretty neat, because I didn't make as much as the test inspectors and was looking forward to the big raise I was going to get as a result of this new assignment. Up till now this job was necessary for my growth and any future promotions, etc., etc., crap. They desperately needed someone with my supervisory experience to straighten out the bad guys in the test rooms, etc. This was the line of shit they tried to run by me to convince me that I wasn't being punished for my remarks to the big guy when everyone in the organization, from the clerks to the other supervisors, knew the real reason.

Armed with my knowledge of the pay scale discrepancy and company policy, I sought out my boss to tell him how grateful I

37

was to have the chance to work on the second shift and even happier to be getting the big raise that would put me 25 percent over my five top-rated employees. I said I just knew that they were doing this on purpose because times were tough and they had already told most of us that we wouldn't be receiving merit raises and this was his way of assuring that I would at least get that much money. I thanked him and walked away. Sometimes, when I would stoop to taking advantage of people who were obviously dumber than I was (which was an achievement in itself), I would feel bad. But not for long and not too often. I mean that three of them had gotten together and tried to figure out the worst thing they could do to me, and as it turned out, I was just a touch smarter than the three of them together, so why should I feel bad? I didn't.

Well, it didn't take them more than two days to figure out that if they left me there I would get the money, as I had already compiled the paperwork and submitted it to the clerk for their approvals, so they had to come up with a new ''cover'' story to suit the crime and transferred me to the midnight shift (12:00 A.M. to 8:00 A.M. with a paid lunch) and told me to work with the repair guys. This was a great job, as there was no production to run and no big guys around to tell you how to do your job! The repair guys needed an experienced supervisor, and the second-shift test guys could wait to be straightened out when my medical restriction was removed in six or seven months. No problem!

6

Pyrotechnic Engineering

by Les Wheeler

A strange term, *pyrotechnic engineering*, in layman's terms it translates to "fire fighting." To those of you that don't work in the industry, it means putting out fires, the fires that pop up when the system doesn't work like it's supposed to. Something, somewhere, fails and two parts don't fit together like they did in the test lab or like the blueprint says they should, and you have to try some problem solving techniques to resolve the situation. Often in the heat of battle (and it is a war zone out there some days), it is easy to forget your basic problem solving techniques, which call for you to identify the problem, then quick-fix it if you can (a quick fix is like sticking your finger in the dike: it works for a while, but the hole is still there and if you remove your finger the leak starts again, often worse than before because your finger made the hole bigger), find the root cause of the problem, take some permanent corrective action on the root cause, and then prevent it from happening again. An example of this is if you were sent to drain a swamp full of alligators, the quick fix would be to shoot the alligators. The next step of permanent corrective action would be to drain the swamp, thus denying the alligators a home. Prevention would be paving the swamp, thus preventing the alligators from returning. No swamp, no alligators. Sounds real simple, doesn't it? In real life, it doesn't always work that way. In real life, sometimes we get so wrapped up with shooting the alligators (quick fix) that we forget the objective was to drain the swamp! We sometimes forget why we were sent here in the first place and just keep on shooting, or sometimes there are so many alligators that we never get to the original objective of draining the swamp. That's where management is supposed to help. They should be aware enough to see what is or isn't going on with the situation at least enough to realize that the swamp isn't getting drained and that the alligators are winning. If that's the case, you need more help or something to turn the tide in favor of the good guys. It doesn't happen that way. The good guys lose sight of the goal and will take a body count of the alligators and assure management that they are winning, not the alligators. Even when the problems still exist, sometimes good news is what you want to hear, and in the face of the truth of the situation we often deny what we see (or are told) because we don't want to deal with the problem. So, we let the quick fix be the answer because it looks good on paper and maybe the problem has abated enough to be a minor fire compared to what it was yesterday and looks better now than it did then.

So, what do we breed when we deal with problems like this? We breed "pyrotechnic engineers": people who are experts at quick fixes and moving on to their next job while hoping that the same problem doesn't pop up again while they are still in the area. Sometimes even when it does, pyrotechnic engineers can always say that it was fixed once and if you had just followed their game plan, it would still be OK, enough said. It doesn't pay to really try to resolve the problem forever, because that's not what they reward or recognize you for. Nobody gets raises or promotions for preventing problems; you get them for being a hero by fire fighting. That's the answer to getting to the top or getting raises: superficial answers to deep problems that ensure that the problems will always be problems. We used to laugh that we could keep a log of daily problems and if we kept it long enough, we could predict when the next problem would pop up and correct it before it did occur. This would mean fewer petty problems and more time to work on real system problems that were crippling our efforts to improve our quality, reduce our costs, and satisfy the customer all at once. The problem with this kind of thinking is that it was coming from outside the circle. It was foreign to the culture of firefighters, and they just couldn't change their paradigms to allow for this new thought process. It was against everything they stood for (and against) and could cause them to lose their power if they didn't play their cards right.

The pace of working in an environment where only fire fighting is encouraged can be horrific at times. The good ones can keep up the pace seemingly forever. That's on the outside. Things are often quite different on the inside. Too often, when you have to work at that kind of pace, the people who can't keep it up start to drop off procedures that they shouldn't because they don't have time to do it right. Or they start to cut corners that they shouldn't, and pretty soon chaos reigns. It becomes a way of life where it didn't exist before, and as long as we don't fight back with long-term system changes, it stays that way forever, or at least it seems like forever. It seems like a life sentence in a strange kind of hell that we made for ourselves. You can try to get out, but if you do try, there is some asshole who thinks you are after his job and will go out of his way to sabotage your efforts. That may sound too hard to believe, but it happens all the time. The problem is that people often think you are after their jobs when all you really want is to escape the day-to-day problems and make it easier for yourself. That shouldn't be too hard to deal with, but it is, especially if they got their job by screwing someone else out of it. Let me give you some examples of how this works.

I was working in a machining area and just trying to do the best I could. I had started to make some headway at my new assignment when the big boss changed my supervisor. My new supervisor, I found out later, felt very threatened by me and took some steps to make sure that I wasn't looked on too favorably or more fondly by the big boss than he was. It's really too easy to do this, much more easy than you might think. He just waited until about two hours after the shift had started, went to the big boss, and asked if she had seen me today. Very innocent question, when you think about it, as every supervisor should have the right to know where his people are, right? The only problem was that he told her that he had been looking for me, hadn't seen me, and was wondering if perhaps, just perhaps, she had sent me somewhere else outside of the plant and forgotten to tell him. Sounded like he had been looking for me everywhere and I was nowhere to be found. To the uninitiated, you might think I was out screwing off somewhere where I shouldn't have been, because he had been looking for me everywhere. I mean he just said he was, didn't he? Unfortunately, he neglected to tell her that he had looked for me in places where I wasn't supposed to be, like in the cafeteria, in the material offices, out on the receiving dock, downstairs in the tool room, across the street in another area, or, if you follow this line of thinking, anywhere but where I was supposed to be. So, when you think about it, he really was telling the truth. Not the whole truth, but just enough of it that he could look her in the eye and not really be lying. This tactic can be quite effective if you practice it long enough. Neat trick, huh?

Well, needless to say, I was called on the phone and ordered to present myself to the big boss as soon as possible, which I did, not knowing why or for what. I then proceeded to get most of my butt chewed off, before I could even utter one syllable in my defense. It would have been pretty futile to try to defend myself anyway, as the boss had already formed an opinion and any attempt by me to bring any sanity or truth to the situation would have been hopeless at this point. You may have heard the old adage ''the first liar wins . . .''; this is how it originated.

It would be one thing if this were an isolated incident along the path of life, but it wasn't, or should we say it isn't? It happens with all too much regularity and frequency to be an isolated incident. It is a way of life, because the powers that are in promote, reward, and recognize their own kind. I've heard it said (and it's true) that people often look like their dogs, and this is the same theory. You tend to promote people that most "look" like you. So, if you're in, you keep promoting people who aspire to your ideals, such as they are, even when they are the wrong ones. People never move forward the careers of "outsiders," as their views are too different, even when they are right. That's the paradigm problem we talked about earlier. If your paradigm is "THE" paradigm, then nothing ever really changes. It really can't, because no one can see a new one. They all think alike, and that's part of the problem within General Motors. From the top to the bottom, if you don't hold the party line, it won't fly. The phrase *not invented here* was invented to cover this dilemma: "It couldn't have been invented here, or we would have thought of it before you did." I hate to say it, but I will: too often we were right and they then had to be wrong. We didn't do that by chance; we just paid attention to what was going on and when things changed we weren't trying to find what was wrong, but what was right.

In reality, it didn't take mental giants or rocket scientists; it simply took someone who would listen and react, the key word being *listen*. Anyone could react and in most cases they over-reacted. Too often they reacted without listening or in spite of what they heard. In spite of, because too often it was different from what they wanted to hear and, consequently, they couldn't hear it or see it. It is still happening today, or H. Ross Perot would still be on the board and we wouldn't have spent $750 million to get him off the board and keep him quiet. He was a commonsense kind of guy who could see some of the wrongs within and couldn't go along with the party line. He had to point out what was wrong as he saw it. The only problem was that they couldn't see the same problems he could, because they all had the same paradigms. Unfortunately, that can often lead to a terminal case of certainty, and it may have by the time this gets to print and you can read it. It may not be as funny if it's viewed as a post-mortem of what went wrong within and not be a comedy, but a tragedy, and that's what it is, a tragedy that we let happen to the greatest company in the world.

In the final analysis, the problem was too many big guys grasping for power instead of trying to make the company greater. Too many big guys trying to intimidate others into doing it their way instead of the right way, trying to misuse the system at the expense of the company and eventually scuttling the monster within. Unfortunately for them, there will never be enough toilet paper in the world to dry the tears of the people they destroyed on their path to the destruction of this great company. Too many of these guys knew every in and out of misusing the system.

It is still a power grab even as the doors are shutting on their asses as the ship goes down. It is almost as if they would still be winners if they had the most toys (power) while the water was lapping at their heels. Keeping in mind, of course, that as the water laps at their heels, it is already over our heads.

7

We Weren't Angels

by Rino Pagnucco

You know, it's amazing; throughout history it seems like there has always been sex, drugs, and other sorts of entertainment. In my case, it was rock-'n'-roll. In 1964, when I hired in with General Motors, I was a new very happily married man. I would have never guessed that the movies *Bob & Ted & Carol & Alice* and *The Graduate* would somehow end up as part of my lifestyle. I would sit there with my wife (ex-wife now) and say, "Gee, how could they do that?" I would have never thought that I would smoke marijuana. Not a lot, but at a party to show everyone that I was part of the "in crowd" or, as the later years turned out, as a means of getting sex. Not like some people in government who say they never "inhaled." My problem was that when I did smoke a joint, I got so damn hungry I just had to eat everything in the refrigerator, even the stuff I didn't like. One time, I found myself eating liverwurst. I hate liverwurst! So I just used pot when I found out a certain woman that I wanted to date liked it. It was a means, or a tool, for getting to the sexual part of the evening, the same way alcohol might be used. The other reason I had to give up the weed was that after smoking a joint with the woman I wanted to have sex with, when we were finally having sex, during the sex, she thought I was having an orgasm, but I was really having a "pizza attack." Sex was too important to

45

me. Hey, I'm Italian; it's a tradition. The "herb" had to go. I mean, I would have it around, just in case someone wanted it, but I would stick with a glass of wine or my Southern Comfort "Dry" Manhattan and resume the chase.

I couldn't say life would be any different if I hadn't worked in the factories, because we all saw this same type of behavior in our everyday lives, no matter how much money you had or didn't have, and it made no difference where you worked. Like every other story you have heard, it starts out innocently and, as it continues, becomes a problem. Sometimes, it can become obsessive and dangerous. When I first saw the movie *Fatal Attraction* (1987), I said to myself, *My God, this has happened to others.* I never thought I would stop for a beer after work at a bar. I mean, what for? I had beer at home, I had a family at home, I was happily married, and I was happy with my life. Sometimes you just have to do it. I guess I thought it was the thing to do. Besides, you're the man of the family, your dad did it, his dad did it, and now it's your turn. If your wife gets upset, now you do it just for spite: "I'll show her who runs this household." What a bunch of bullshit that turned out to be. Now, not only does the drinking away from home occur, but it's accompanied by the "companionship" of someone else, usually the opposite sex, who "understands" what you are going through but becomes part of the problem. You must understand that you do not have to be into drugs or drinking to get into these situations. Somehow it evolves, harmlessly at a party, or with an eye glance as you pass by in the aisleway or at some fun function with friends the seed is planted.

The problem in the late sixties and seventies was that this type of behavior was not frowned upon. It was almost looked at as being OK, the "in" thing to do. Drinking after work with the boys or finding out where the bosses went to drink and going there was acceptable. You would say to yourself, *I'll show them. If they can drink and chase women after work and it's OK, well, so can I.* It seemed to be OK. It was almost the accepted thing to do, as long as you didn't embarrass anyone from the plant or the office where you worked. It really went from an occasional drink after work with the boys at a place called Bobby's to an occasional drink at night with the guys. This led to having a good time with the guys and gals from work or wherever to an occasional "harmless" date with other women. Just drinking and dancing and good times, nothing serious. Well, after a little harping by wifey, you start saying, "She doesn't understand," and the date you're dancing and drinking with now looks even better, because she "understands." I mean, she is at work and sees what kind of problems you have to put up with. She really understands. Well, all of a sudden, it's "wham, bam, thank you, ma'am." Wow, you feel like a man. You, Mr. "STUD MAN," just scored. Just like in the movies. But you also feel like a piece of crap. You're driving home, it's late, and you keep thinking to yourself, *Boy, it sure felt good at the time, but I don't want to lose what I already have. I really don't have it that bad.*

This guilt trip is about to be a journey you will never forget. It will be compromised by lies and more lies. It's your job now to keep track of your lies. For the first time in your married life, you hope like hell your spouse doesn't want to fool around when you get home. What's going through your mind is that all of this is really wrong and you have to stop. You have yourself convinced of this. But when you get in to work, everyone is looking at you, not because you did something that you should be ashamed of, but as a "HERO." Hell, you "SCORED." What a guy! Your bosses would know, and they would smile at you, pat you on the back, and maybe say, "Looks like no woman is safe out there when you go out," or, "All you Italians are alike," still patting you on the back and smiling as if to say, "We have accepted you as part of us; welcome to the gang; keep up the fine work." If you went out into the assembly line, it was like everyone knew and you would be walking and everyone would be silently cheering. As you walk farther, you pass the young lady you had sex with last night and she looks even better than ever. My friend, you are "hooked"! You're a done deal! You are an addict, not to drugs or alcohol, but to the lifestyle of the times.

Alcohol was, and still is, a very large problem in the workplace, if not the number-one problem. Drugs are definitely in the workplace. Alcohol and marijuana are usually found in the areas where overtime is not plentiful, like assembly lines and subassembly areas. Cocaine and other high-dollar drugs are found more in the high overtime areas like machining operations or nine-and-ten-hour-a-day operations that work six and seven days a week. It's only natural that cocaine and the bigger drugs go with the bigger bucks.

Sex is still a problem at the workplace, but not as much. Basically because of the AIDS virus and the upturn in sexual harassment cases. See, at one time, your raise or promotion or some other sort of "special treatment" depended on who you went out with. Some of the really easy jobs on the assembly line were, amazingly, held by women. That was sometimes dependent on whom they went to bed with. It gets even better. We had committeemen and union officials that helped their daughters, wives, or girlfriends get hired in; then they also got some special treatment. It was like cancer; it kept spreading until it just got out of control. There were many women who were very attractive and still had morals. They wouldn't have sex or play these silly games with certain people and, in return, they found themselves on some very undesirable jobs. They would either finally "come across" or be transferred or even be fired. Not all but most of these women were divorced and needed a job. A factory job was a very good-paying job, packaged with some pretty nice benefits. Most of these women had small children, and their so-called low-life, cheating, scum-bag, good-for-nothing husbands, who got caught screwing someone else, weren't giving up any money. So, the benefits were a big financial help. Whether you were in the front offices or in the assembly lines in the back, the same situations happened every day.

Even though the automobile companies put a tremendous amount of money into programs to help alcoholics, drug addicts, and folks with family problems and other personal problems, they still don't like to say they have a problem. Here's how it works. If a plant manager says he has a problem with any of the above situations, the plant is looked upon as one with a whole lot of problems and that, therefore, must be mismanaged. So, here is what they do. They just say, "We don't have those kind of problems here. We have some, but nothing to really worry about." So, therefore, you have . . . no problems.

Situations occurred in our plant that you could set your watch to. You knew it was ten or fifteen minutes before break time or lunchtime when you saw certain groups of people leaving the work site. I don't mean just their job area; I mean going out to their cars and leaving the parking lot. They would leave before anyone else and come back after everyone else, and come back "happier" than everyone else. You've got to believe they were doing more than reading *Playboy* or *Playgirl* in their cars. I mean, come on; their cheeks were a little rosier and their eyes were a little bit glassier than normal. Then everyone starts making jokes like, "Hey, why don't we just move the department over to the corner on Ecorse Road where the party store is? We would get more production!" This way they wouldn't have to get into their cars and travel back and forth. They could just go over to the cooler and grab a cold one! These are usually the same people that are heavy union supporters, and the union will support these people. Though I did see that the unions are getting very tired of bailing out the same troublemakers and are starting to say, "We've got programs; get some help or we are not going to help you anymore.'' Management still won't get into a pissing contest with the union on these issues because, again, this would mean we have a problem.

Let me say something about the "union representatives" here, also known as shop stewards, committeemen, or committee persons. They are the hourly person's "lawyers." They know the current contract better than most supervisors do. That is their job, their only job. That's why they are good at it. They study the contract all day, the union sends them to schools, and, of course, the company pays for it. Kind of ironic, isn't it? When I say it is like our judicial system, I mean, think of it this way. We catch the criminals, we put them in prison, in prison they study the law and get a degree and then turn around, while still in prison, and sue society for fucking with them, and they win! By no means am I insinuating that union representatives are criminals or anything like that. I'm just comparing society paying for the criminal to become a lawyer with the company paying the union representative to become a lawyer. The grievance procedure in the plants and office complexes, where hourly people work, is also very similar to the judicial system in our society. They have come a long way. There are "umpire" decisions that are about many thousands of dollars and can set precedents on future contract talks. These umpires are not from the company or the union; they are outside lawyers and judges that are paid equally by both sides. Now the supervisor on the floor has to wear many hats and do many jobs and, since we are doing comparisons, is similar to a "cop." His school training (street smarts) is usually acquired when discipline is necessary on the plant floor as if you were a cop on the street.

In my last year in manufacturing, I was put into an area that had the nickname of Cocaine Alley. Now, I would think that this might give you an indication that coloring books of Walt Disney characters wasn't the favorite pastime here. When I first went there, I had some secret meetings with higher management and plant security about what was going on and how we were going to make an attempt to stop the majority, if not all, of the drug problems in the area. There was a lot of support and hard work by a lot of people to try to clean up this mess. When my car was threatened with being blown up, higher management let me park it in a restricted area inside the plant. The plant manager even came down to see me and offered his support, to the hilt, if it meant getting rid of drugs. But when it was time for the action to happen, everybody was too busy or it was the wrong time for them. It was never said, but management's theory of not going forward with this drug raid was that they were trying to get new business in the plant. They were trying to keep it open and not make it one of the plants that General Motors was going to close. So, if we said we had a drug problem, it would possibly make us look bad in the eyes of the people downtown and this might hurt our chances of staying open.

Well, it worked. I was frustrated to no end; they still had the drug problem; they got rid of me and still kept the plant open. I mean they (higher management) were happy that General Motors chose the plant to stay open and the druggies were happy to see me go away.

There was one time when a particular superintendent told me to fire this one guy. This hourly person was truly an asshole and a troublemaker. Many of the hourly people didn't have any use for this guy either. Well anyway, the superintendent told me to make up a reason, any reason, and fire him! They would get enough witnesses to back up any story I came up with. When the superintendent found out one night that there was an incident in the plant that involved this guy and I didn't fire him, he called me on the phone. There wasn't enough proof of wrongdoing to fire the guy, but there was enough to give him substantial time off without pay, which I did. Well, that wasn't good enough; that superintendent called me every name he could think of that started with the word *fuck* because I told him I wasn't going to make up some story to fire this guy. I told him it would be just a matter of time and he would be fired legally. The superintendent and I never talked after that incident. He went on to a different area and shortly afterward left the plant, and so did I. About a year after that, I heard the hourly guy finally quit. Why didn't they set him up after I left? Maybe I was being set up!

I am not without guilt here. I have seen my own workers drunk and obnoxious and did nothing because of not having enough people to cover their job if I threw them out. At one time, you, as a supervisor, could remove someone that was drunk or high without too much of a problem. Everyone, including the committeeman, would know who these people would be, because they were normally the repeat offenders. The union got smarter and started saying things like, "Are you a doctor?" or: "What makes you such an authority on knowing when someone is under the influence of alcohol or high on drugs?"

Well, when these cases got to Labor Relations, they were lost. There were a couple of reasons for this. One, inexperienced labor representatives that had never faced the actual everyday, on-the-floor situations as supervisors. I mean if you have never been in a situation where a drunk employee is standing on top of your desk, in the middle of your department, calling you a motherfucker at the top of his lungs and saying that your mother is a whore, waving a three-foot torque wrench, threatening to imbed it in your head or up your rectum, possibly both, and also now has stopped production, you really haven't had a day in the life of a supervisor. So, you are now trying to tell the labor representative—let's call him Buffy (the son or daughter of someone in higher management)—what just happened. The drunk employee is going to "lie" his ass off, because he knows he is in deep shit. The union representative, the committeeman (or committeeperson), after listening to the employee's story, wants to know why you provoked the employee to the breaking point. Plant security wants to know if they should lie on the report.

Your boss wants to know how you are going to make up the lost production, and all the other employees are saying, "If he comes back, we are all going to get drunk tomorrow." Last, but not least, Buffy, management's answer to a labor representative, feels that if we make the committeeman happy he won't have to do anything else on the case. There is a tremendous amount of paperwork that has to be prepared in these cases. The second reason is that the less Labor Relations has on their agenda, the less ammunition the union has at contract time. Now, the union sees it the other way: the more on the agenda that's not settled, the more trading power they have at negotiations. Buffy doesn't know it, but he or she is in a no-win situation. Politics—both sides use it. Even if you did what you were supposed to do, you would be looked down upon by your bosses because you would have caused a production loss due to the interruption. Another no-win situation. It's easier to cover it up. You did what you were supposed to do. Your boss is saying you did what you were supposed to do . . . kind of . . . because he damn well knows that two weeks from now, no one will really care about the drunk, but they will be on his ass about missing his schedule by the amount of time it took to throw that son of a bitch out of the plant. So, the next time this situation comes up, the questions become: "Well, how drunk is this person? Is this person so high or so much under the influence that he can't run a machine or assemble a part?"

Well, after you have been in this situation a couple of times, you start thinking to yourself, *There is no sense in going through all that fucking hassle and stress. I'll just leave the employee on the job, hope for the best, and get on with my day.* You just hope that somewhere down the line quality won't be sacrificed due to this action.

Most of us have seen the sixties, seventies, and eighties come and go. Unfortunately, the nineties, in many ways, have made a full circle in the issues of sex, drugs, and rock-'n'-roll.

The amount of publicity AIDS, sex, drugs, and alcohol have generated is very high, but these are still major problems at our work sites and our schools, as they were thirty years ago. Only now a lot more people are dying from it.

8

Sex, Drugs, and Rock-'n'-Roll

by Les Wheeler

In the Big D, as in Detroit, where Rino and I come from, the above is the answer to the question: "Why is there life?" But if you took enough of the middle one, you could always remember the answers, but never the question. This was sort of a joke we all used whenever things got too bad to deal with. You know, like when reality rears its ugly head and just too much shit is going down to deal with. I'm sure you have had days like that yourself. Someone would spout out the answers and then complain that he couldn't remember the questions, and everyone else would seize the moment to relax just a little, no matter how hot the situation. It's amazing how much humor helps in the most trying times. It's also amazing just how much upper management hates anyone who can laugh in the fact of impending disaster. We can actually recall people telling us that we obviously did not understand the seriousness of the problem if we could jest at a time like this. We often told the members of upper management that if we didn't laugh at the seriousness of the situation, that only left one other option, and we hated to cry at work in front of our employees. Somehow, that comment was lost on them, too. It seemed to suffer somewhat in the translation from reality to the dreamworld they lived in.

Speaking of dreamworlds, one superintendent I worked for was right up there among the top dogs of not seeing the humor in much of anything, let alone trying to see the bright side of impending doom. He fancied himself to be the leader in any "new" idea he might come across in his travels through wherever his head might go. Let me point out that many times we were accused of being on drugs or suspected of the same. Many times I suspected upper management of being on either drugs or alcohol, because of their actions and words, more than I suspected known drug users of being the proverbial "one toke over the line" at work. To be sure, some of these fine fellows, including me, partied hearty when the time was right. But that was after work and in the right company, certainly never while on the job, during lunch, or just prior to coming in. When I did party, which was fairly frequently, the drug of choice was beer, cold, wet, and lots of them. Preferably in that order and then close together. Like you would be opening one while you were putting one down, if you know what I mean.

Anyway, this superintendent would take a class in Bible reading, find religion, and the next thing you knew, the whole damn department would be "asked" to attend Bible reading meetings during lunch or after work in this guy's office. Interestingly enough, some of these bozos would actually give up their lunch to spend this time pretending to enjoy reading the Bible with the boss. Talk about your basic suckasses. I'm telling you, it was nauseating to anyone else who managed to maintain any sense of sanity in the face of these do-gooders. Strange as it may seem, they never seemed to grasp just how unbelievable this was to anyone else around them. Now I'm not, in any way, knocking religious people. I had many churchgoers work for me, in probably every department I ever supervised, but it wasn't the "program of the month" type I'm talking about here. I'm not going to talk about people who believed what they found in the teachings of the Bible and religion and actually treated others the way they would like to be treated and didn't run around on their spouses or go out drinking every night or take drugs at work, etc. No, I'm talking about the guys who read the Bible at lunch and then go out to lunch, even though they just supposedly used it up, to have a few drinks, make loud lewd remarks to the poor waitress who happened to have to wait on their table, and then plan on how to screw over the first supervisor (or hourly employee) they came into contact with after lunch. I think the word that would best describe their behavior is *hypocritical*. If they really believed, that would be one thing, but that never really entered their minds, nor anyone else's for that matter. Of course, those of us that had the pleasure of working for them had to pretend that they were, in fact, real good guys when, in fact, we all knew better but had to play the game. Some guys played it a little harder than the rest of us and sat in on these meetings whenever they could to try to get that one little step up on anyone else when it came time for the next promotion. Great guys to be around. If they weren't stabbing you in the back, they were holding the knife for someone else. Personally, Rino and I could never stoop to such antics. For one reason: we both had bad backs and stooping was out of the question for either of us. For another reason: we both had to shave in the morning and we could never figure out how anyone could suck up to someone or stab or help stab someone in the back to further his own career and then look himself in the face the next day when he shaved. To this day, it's still a mystery that will forever remain unanswered. Bummer!

Usually, these phases only lasted for a couple of months before reverting back to the old behaviors followed. The fun part of watching all this unfold in front of you was that the suckies would sometimes not see the demise of one phase and the birth of the new one. This was really great, as you could see them still carrying their Bibles around, waiting for the next meeting, when the new show in town was skeet shooting after work.

Believe it or not, the new game in town once was skeet shooting. My boss asked me to get involved, be a part of the inspection team, and actually go out and purchase a new shotgun and whatever else one would need to partake of the fine sport of destroying innocent skeets. Well, I told him that, for one thing, I didn't trust myself (nor should he trust me) that close to him or his boss with a loaded gun in my hands after the way they had been treating me for the last several months. Needless to say, they never broached the subject again with me, although I understand that I was the talk of the luncheon meetings for quite some time after that. It seems that every aspect of my personnel file and my personal life was being explored in the hopes of finding something they could fire me for.

Once the superintendent took an introductory class in psychology and thought he was Sigmund Freud for the next three months. What a trip for those of us around him. Let me qualify the following with the statement that I (while certainly making no claim to any real psychological ability) had already taken over sixteen hours in psychology courses at Wayne State University. So, I really wasn't too taken in by his sudden expertise in the field. I didn't know much, but I certainly knew better. So did some of the other guys, but they wouldn't say shit if their mouth was full of it either. Anyway, this superintendent had a picture of a pumpkin field, and in this field was an unlucky pumpkin, which happened to be growing inside a bottle. As you might guess, this poor pumpkin could never grow to its full potential as long as it was in the jar. We're talking some real heavy thought patterns here, aren't we, folks? So, this guy had all of his general supervisors and then each of the supervisors come in his office to gaze with awe upon the picture of the pumpkin and he would tell them that it represented their career and the possible dead-end job they had, if they didn't expand their perspective on life and their current position.

Really neat stuff, if you had the time or inclination for this kind of drivel, from someone who had no clear idea of what the hell was happening around him. Unfortunately, I had neither the time nor the inclination to listen or to even pretend I was listening. Sure, you might say, anyone can find the time if he wants to. But if you have never worked as a supervisor on an assembly line during the late sixties and early seventies, it's difficult to understand the time constraints we worked within. Not only did the work line itself give you problems, but so did the people, and your boss was no help, as he often didn't know where the hell the line was, let alone what to do with it if he found it. These were the days of drugs in the workplace, shootings, stabbings, beatings, and whatever.

Well, I was currently enrolled at Wayne State and attending classes four nights a week and I knew this jerk was going to tell me that I should go back to school to better myself. Great. What kind of superintendent are you if you don't even know who is doing just that works for you? Or maybe he knew and was going to prove to me just how smart he was after taking his one class. I still don't know, nor do I care. So, when I got the opportunity to sit in the great one's office and listen to the speech, I was ready and waiting. I had already heard what was going on and, although I didn't believe everything I heard, this one sounded too weird to not be true. Well, there I am and the superintendent gets up and shuts the door behind me. We sit down and both stare at the pumpkin on the wall. He looks at me and says, ''Well, what do you think of the picture?''

I look at the picture, I look at him, I look at the picture again, I swallow hard, and I say, ''Do you really want to know?''

Of course, he falls for my trap and says, ''Yes, I really want you to level with me on what you think of the picture.''

So, being the asshole that I am, I told him, ''It looks like it needs more orange.''

I couldn't believe the shade of orange he turned at that moment. What I wouldn't have given for a movie camera at the time! Well, he stayed that shade of orange for longer than, I would have thought, anyone could and not explode. He looked at me and then got up, went to his door, and opened it as he turned back toward me and calmly told me to "get the fuck out of my office and never come into it again as long as either of us live."

So, I got up, went to the door, turned slowly, and said, "Well, I asked if you wanted to know and you said you did." I had a few other comments to share with him, but the look he gave me suggested that I should leave now and keep these to myself. As it was, I worried that he might explode and I would be charged with manslaughter or something, so I left. Hey, at least I lived to fight another day.

Earlier in this chapter, I suggested that there might be a double standard in how things were run in the organization. The so-called big guys, like the superintendents and general foremen, had their own rules, but the rest of us lived by an entirely different set. I suppose you could say that the old "RHIP" (Rank Has Its Privileges) theory applies here. But it was usually carried a little beyond that theory. Take, for instance, lunch. Lunch was usually from 10:30 to 11:00 A.M. That's not as early as it sounds. If you start work at 6:00 in the morning, 10:30 A.M. is not a bad time to eat lunch. Amazingly enough, every bar in the area would open at 10:00 A.M. just in case anyone got out early for lunch. Some of the neighborhood establishments would open at 5:30 A.M. to catch a few of the regulars before they went in. What a jolly thought for the supervisors in the plant to know that some of their employees would come in drunk or close to it at 6:00 A.M.! What a fun way to start one's day! These bars would also be ready and waiting for the guys that worked the midnight shift and got off work at 8:00 A.M. We're not saying that the bars were at fault, any more than the guys who drank there. It's just a fact of life. Working on the line every day is not a fun job, even if you happened to have a good one, and there weren't many of those around either.

Anyway, it was a problem in some areas that there wasn't anyone around at 10:30 A.M. to stop the line when the lunch whistle blew. Nor was there anyone around to turn it back on when lunch was over. Slight problem, which was easily overcome. You just had to draw straws, and sooner or later it was your turn to stick around and turn the line off and then back on again. A tough job, but somebody had to do it! The problem was that some areas couldn't even agree on that. Such teamwork the world has never seen. It is kind of tough to convince your hourly employees to stay in the area when some groups couldn't even keep their own supervisors on the job until the whistle blew. In our cases, we were not saints or martyrs either. We liked to leave a little early now and then, too. But the point we always tried to make to our guys was: "You stay until you see me leave, and then don't pass me in the aisle." Fairly simple rule. Fairly simple results. Our people stayed until we left and then didn't pass us in the aisle. If someone had to do something special at lunch, that might take a few extra minutes, all he had to do was ask and make a good case and not every day and things like this could happen. The problem came when the big guys would get a bug, somewhere the sun don't shine, and want to crack down on everybody. Strange as it may seem to you, the chronic abusers of the policies rarely got caught up in this activity, because they were usually gone before the big guys came out of their offices, and even stranger is that it seemed that everyone but them knew they were doing this. We kind of think they knew it but ignored the fact.

Well, there they were, out on the floor, worrying about someone leaving two minutes early for lunch, someone who had been working well all morning including, for that matter, as you knew since you had been in the area, when the supervisors from the same area had already been gone for thirty minutes before the big guys showed up. Keep in mind that everyone in the area knew this but them, and we still think they knew but pretended ignorance. In behalf of some of them, let us state that ignorance for some of them was no stretch. Ignorance was, in some cases, seen to be a key characteristic in their job descriptions. Not only would they try to impress you and anyone else around that they reigned supreme over the troops and you, but they would try to point it out by the silly enforcement of rules that they didn't think were important enough for them to follow. They were only important for the "troops" to follow. Don't get us wrong here. We think the rules were there to be followed. But by everyone, not just the guys who were already working hard anyway.

We've both been in areas where the rules were followed by everyone, from the sweeper to the superintendent, and we can both vouch for the fact that these areas were the easiest to work in. Everyone knew the rules and anyone could see that the rules were for everyone, not just for some. If a supervisor took advantage of the rules, he would hear about it just as quick as the hourly employee. When the rules are made clear and don't favor one group over another, you don't have problems. People like to have some order in their lives. They also like to have that order apply to everyone doing the same basic jobs, hourly or salary.

Now, if someone is yelling at me to yell at someone else when others have already violated the rules by a long shot and no one is or will be concerned with them, now or later, does it make for good discipline, good relations, or just plain good common business sense to do it? Of course not. But even this would be sort of excusable if it ended here. Unfortunately, it doesn't. The big guys would come out, disrupt whatever relations you might have going or been trying to get going, stir up the pot, and then go to lunch. Remember, lunch is from 10:30 to 11:00 A.M. They would get off their duffs for five minutes before lunch and then go back to their office until 11:00 A.M., when they would come out again to see who would come back late. It was not a fun time of the day for any supervisors trying to do the right thing. Again, it's not that we are proposing that people do the wrong things; it was suggested that they clean up the real bad guys before messing with the penny-ante characters. It's kind of like the IRS. If you owe them $2 million, they will settle for ten cents on the dollar and set up a payment plan. But if you owe them $500, they want it tomorrow and they ain't taking no guff either.

It is only in recent times that some of the double standards within General Motors are starting to be eliminated. In some areas they still flourish, but in many others they are slowly, but surely, becoming like the dinosaurs that are still trying to cling to them. We see less and less "class" type distinctions, such as parking privileges, color backgrounds by level on your identification badge, and dress codes. It is way past time for all of them, but in the giant it's tough to break from the past, even in the light of day.

The life of a supervisor, on any assembly line, is spent in the fast lane for the full eight hours of every day. If it's not one thing, it's seven others. They all seem to go wrong at the most inopportune time possible. In any given day, it could be that not enough people showed up for work to start the line or to run tag relief (tag relief means that you don't have to stop the line for break time, as you have enough extra people to send some of them on break and still run the line, so you can make more engines, or whatever, without stop; which is tougher on the supervisors and the workers but does allow better use of the facilities), it could be that you don't have enough parts on hand to run the schedule, but generally we ran the line anyway and put the engines in the "hole" (the off-line repair area, whose name probably derived from the fact that many engines that went to repair ended up in a "black hole" from which they never returned). We actually inventoried the same engine two years in a row, in two different locations of the plant. The customer never got the first one, so we rescheduled it, ran it again, and still never shipped it. Luckily, the customer was the Navy or they might have really been pissed that we were so late with the order! God knows what they wanted the engine for, but it couldn't have been a really high priority. Rumor had it that this engine had been moved so much in the plant that it was out of warranty before the Navy received it!

We got so good at running engines without parts that we invented "SSBO" rules. "SSBO" stands for "Ship Short—Back Order." Some materials department people got so good at the "rules" (there were actually no written rules), an overzealous material supervisor trying to make his count for the day would authorize SSBO on internal parts. This, of course, meant that the engine couldn't be tested, or when the customer received it, it couldn't be used until the parts showed up, which could be a long time down the road. This is hardly the way to satisfy customers, but in those days, we weren't as interested in satisfying customers as we were in meeting the schedules. I knew of an instance where we actually had only seven parts to build ten engines. So, the material guys would wait until the engine was built, put it on the dolly to go to Engine Test, then take off the part and return it to the assembly area to be put on the next engine. If I hadn't had some knowledge of the shortage, three customers would have received engines missing some external components and would, most likely, have been really upset.

This was just one example of where schedule beat the pants off of quality. We used to make the comparison of quality and quantity all the time. There were only two letters' difference in the words, but it made all the difference in the world to the customers. Back then, we obviously never knew what we were talking about or, to quote the big guys, "You just don't see the big picture." They also used the line, "You're just not a team player," whenever you raised any questions about shipping poor-

or low-quality engines. These mental giants very nearly succeeded in putting Detroit Diesel out of business, because of its well-deserved reputation for poor quality. Poor quality was the disease; the things we are talking about were only the symptoms.

Living in the so-called fast lane placed one heck of a lot of stress on the best of supervisors and even more on the poor devil who got the job because of who he knew, not what he might know. Sometimes it seemed like you make two thousand decisions a day minimum, then, when you got home, your wife would ask what you wanted for dinner and bad shit would happen. It seemed like most wives couldn't or wouldn't try to understand that you were decisioned out for the day and didn't really care one way or another what went on the plate, because after most days of two or three packs of cigarettes and God only knows how many cups of black coffee (mainly drunk black, because you didn't usually have the time to put in the fixings), you couldn't taste anything anyway. This would generally end up with: "Hey, stop the bullshit. I get enough of it at work; I don't need it here, too." This was then generally followed by the sound of a door slamming, either the one you slammed on the way out to the nearest bar or the one she slammed as she stormed into the bedroom or wherever she went to hide from you. Many times, it was carried over into the next day or weeks or months and cost you a lot of sorely needed time with someone you really needed but just couldn't get the message to. When you needed her the most, it seemed like she wasn't there. Not to say that it was her fault, but that's the way it usually went down.

One thing you could count on, when things weren't going that great at home, was your fellow supervisors. Odds are they were having the same problems, and you would often run across them at the same bar for the same reasons on any given night. It's better to cry on someone else's shoulder than into your beer to avoid that watered-down taste. There were a lot of waitresses that would listen to your woes, assured that they were different and could soothe your troubles away with a quick roll in the sack and then send you home in hopes that they could nab you for themselves someday. In a lot of cases, unfortunately, that's just how it ended up. Some guys would buckle under to the pressure at work and take to drinking too much, running around with another woman, doing drugs, or any combination of the above and end up in divorce court. The percentage of supervisors who ended up there was way too high when compared to the number who didn't. Sometimes it was just because the pace of the job put you and your spouse so far apart that there wasn't a road back to where you started from. When that happens, what do you do? Where do you go from here?

You wake up one day and need something else and here isn't the place anymore. Being hit at from all sides at work all day is just more than most people are meant to handle. Some of them never get their lives back on track after this. The really sad part is that they were used and abused by the monster (the assembly line itself made a poor mistress, but she was all we had) and whenever it really began to show up with poor attendance, poor work, or whatever, the big guys helped out by getting rid of them like an old shoe. Swell way to do business, but that's how it was. It was one more means of pointing out to the supervisor that the only "real" friends he had were others in the same boat. This was not always the case, but it sure seemed like it at the time.

Right about now seems like a good time to point out a truism from the old days: "One good thing about self-pity, it is sincere if nothing else."

When we talk about drugs, we need to set the stage a little and let you have the background of how many and what drugs were available before we begin to tell the truth that you will probably only read about here. Even as it was becoming an epidemic (yes, we do know what the word *epidemic* means and that's what it was, an epidemic), the big guys were denying that it even existed. The smell of burning rope in the men's rest room, adjacent to the superintendent's office, was not burning rope. It was smoke alright, but not from rope. If you tried to tell someone what it was, he accused you of smoking it yourself, which we can quite honestly say we never did at work. That statement may give you the impression that we smoked it somewhere else or at some other time and that means that we can never be a Supreme Court justice or president of the United States, but what the heck, we didn't want to anyway.

This epidemic would have been bad enough if it was only marijuana. Sad to say, but that was the least of it. There were several drug pushers in the plant during this time frame, and they dealt everything from Mary Jane to heroin. At one time, we figured that there was one major pusher in every building on two shifts. The midnight guys had to do their buying from the day or afternoon guys for a long time. As the number of people on midnights picked up, so did the drug business, and that attracted a pusher or two to the shift. I had, on two separate instances, a drug pusher working in my departments. I can state that I hated what the pushers were doing, but in one case—let's call the guy Tom—he did his job every day and did it well, too. But, unlike some other supervisors, that wasn't enough for me. The drug pushing had to go or he had to go. The problem here was that the same doctor who was denying that we had a drug problem in the plant was doing his "goody two shoes" act and had gotten this guy paroled from Jackson State Prison to me. What a bonus! The doctor only seemed to care about the image General Motors projected about how much they cared about the impoverished and downtrodden souls of society, not the effect that they would have on the environment they were being put into. Tom used to complain to me about the poor quality of the drugs he was using (and dealing) on the outside, as opposed to inside prison. They cost a lot more, too, but then he had more money outside to deal with.

I'll get back to more about Tom later, mainly because there is a lot more to get to. But first, let's finish with the general view of the plant. How bad was it? It was so bad that people overdosed in the rest rooms. Can you imagine looking for an employee and finding him in the men's rest room with a glassy-eyed stare and a needle stuck in his arm? This was something most, if not all, supervisors were unprepared for. It didn't make it any easier when the big guys, at both ends of the plant, denied that the problem even existed. Well, if the problem was a figment of my imagination, then who the hell was that dead guy in the men's rest room? And if he was just a figment, why did a figment smell so bad? I mean you wouldn't think a figment would smell at all, let alone that bad. Just another example of us not seeing the big picture, I guess. Or maybe it was another example of not being team players, but we can tell you for sure the guy in the men's rest room was no figment of anyone's imagination. He was dead and he wasn't ever going to put water pumps on engines again, which, of course, meant that you had to hire another guy to replace him, who may or not be worse than the guy in the rest room, but at least he was warmer. If you get the impression that there wasn't a hell of a lot of time spent in sympathy here, you're right. There wasn't.

9

A Different Kind of Supplier

by Les Wheeler

But let's get back to my drug dealer, Tom. As I said, he was paroled to me from Jackson Prison. He had been serving time for drug-related incidents. He told me that he was busted twice, while in prison, for dealing, distributing, and using. Sounds like a fine candidate for parole, if there ever was one, right? If there was one good thing about Tom, it was the fact that his parole officer would call every week to make sure Tom was at work for every minute of available work. Simply put, that meant that he had to work all forty hours of every week and any overtime that was offered to him. If he missed more than one-tenth of an hour, he had to explain to "THE MAN" why or risk being a parole violator and being sent back to prison. Not a good choice, as he was in some other kind of trouble with someone on the inside for something. I never found out what that something was, but then I never really cared either.

Normally, I would try to find out all that I could about my employees and their families. Birthdays and anniversaries were important events to them, and it helped me, in my job, if I could anticipate a request for a day off to celebrate, especially if they were working one of the two night shifts, afternoons from 3:30 P.M. to 12:00 A.M. or midnights from 11:30 P.M. to 8:00 A.M. I always felt that trying to understand and work with your employees, instead of us versus them, was much easier for both sides. Believe me, that's the way it worked out, too. Somehow, trying to find out anything about Tom's life, such as it was, did not seem to be a high priority to me. It was not that I treated him that much different from anyone else, because I really tried not to, but let's face the reality of it: He *was* different from the others. He was living a lifestyle that assured me that no matter how hard he tried, he was not going to be a long-term employee for me or General Motors. He had fallen back into his old habits and, besides being a dealer, was a user again. You might think that being a user, he might be in violation of his parole, but evidently not. It was certainly important to be at work for every available minute, but not necessarily in condition to work. Somehow, I lose the logic here. I can see where his parole officer was coming from, in that as long as Tom worked every day, he was one less problem for him to deal with. I tried once to clue him in to the real deal here, but he wasn't interested in taking a stand, if he had to be the bad guy. If I wanted to fire Tom for some discipline-related problem, the parole officer would be only too happy to put the clamps on him. Assuming I was still alive, I would have been happy to witness the event. But the kicker was that I had to fire him first. Great choice. The real problem was that I didn't care what imagined thing he might do. I was determined to get him out of the plant and save some others the agonies of heroin use. Tom knew this because I had told him of my intentions during one of our little fireside chats about his job performance and what I expected from him regarding the performance of his job. He did come in every day and he did his job better than most. If he was anyone but a drug dealer, other departments would have robbed me of him months ago. As in a small town, in a plant one's reputation precedes you, and everyone knew of Tom or knew his reputation. So, that kept him with me whether I liked it or not. We did have sort of an arrangement between us.

He would not sell drugs to anyone in my department, and he would not sell drugs during working hours or in his work area. Doesn't sound like much to you, but it was important to me to have some rules. These rules were in place to ease my conscience, not his. As far as I knew, he kept his end of the bargain. But it didn't keep him from selling drugs to anyone else in the plant during his lunch or break time or before or after work.

He was an example to others, as I would often bring youngsters from the area who might be experimenting with social drugs like marijuana or speed and show Tom to them and ask them if they wanted to have swollen arms and legs and tracks up and down their arms when they grew up, too. Tom knew what I was up to and never asked me to stop bringing them by. He knew what he had become but couldn't stop himself. I wanted to help but didn't know how. There was a bridge between us, but one span was down and neither of us knew how to fix it.

Tom once came to me and asked, "If you busted the biggest drug pusher in the plant, would that be a feather in your cap?" My first thought was that he was going to turn himself in and let me get the credit for the bust. This was not the case, but this question did turn into part of one of the most bizarre experiences of my career. Once I determined that he wasn't referring to himself, I told him that it very possibly would be looked at favorably for me. This was, at this point, only a hypothetical conversation that never took place until I could assure him of complete secrecy and promise to maintain his anonymity in the deal. I could barely control my excitement as I assured him that I could guaranty his secrecy and still pull it off. And as far as I was concerned, this conversation had never taken place until I could speak with some degree of certainty to the police, who would obviously have to handle the situation, as I was certain I could not trust internal security to keep it a secret or to pull it off in the first place.

Turns out that I made a good assumption there and gained some of Tom's confidence, as there were some users wearing blue, too. As I didn't approach internal security first, Tom knew that I wasn't as dumb as I looked. So, the first move I took was the right one, for a change anyway.

I talked it over with my supervisor, and even though he knew who my source was, he never once mentioned him by name to me or the police officers who eventually were brought in to do the job. I left it up to my supervisor to contact the local police department and keep me out of the picture until they needed to know me. All the police knew was that a drug bust could be had for the asking if they wanted it. All they had to do was to figure out who had jurisdiction and then say yes. Until then, I was kept out of the limelight. That included my identity as much as Tom's. We figured the less people who knew about me, the better for me and for the bust and for keeping my source's identity a secret. They never knew who my source was, and only two undercover officers knew who I was. So it didn't look like we couldn't pull it off.

The jurisdiction part was kind of interesting, as the personnel offices of the plant and all administrative functions were in Detroit. The rest of the plant was in a city called Redford Township. So who would handle the bust was up to them. They decided that since the bust would most likely take place in the engine assembly area (in Redford), they would handle all the details. This was fine by me, as I knew some guys on the Redford force and they were death on drug pushers. Also fine by me.

The whole damn deal was very stressful for me and for Tom, as it took longer to set the bust up and that meant longer to maintain the secrecy than either of us liked. I was pretty sure that I was the only person involved in the whole scenario who wasn't carrying a gun. I had always had my suspicions that Tom was packing one but was never sure. I was sure that the two guys from the force were and suspected that the individual we (they) were going to nab would be carrying more than drugs when the deal went down.

My part in the bust would be to maintain Tom's identity, to keep that secret, no matter how the bust went and to signal the police when to make the hit, based on my source. Tom was going to tell me when the dealer had the drugs on him in a large-enough quantity to make the bust worthwhile and when he could be sure that any suspicion would not be solely on him. If there was some doubt as to who put the finger on him, there was no doubt that he would try to kill or have everyone he suspected killed. I could appreciate the logic here, as I didn't want to be fingered either.

After weeks of setting up the details, signals, and whatever, the big day finally arrived. I got the word from my guy and gave the word to the police. They did a nice job on the collar, and I'll bet that not three people in the area knew that something had indeed gone down. I appreciated the secrecy about my part in it, and Tom appreciated the secrecy about his role as there were no repercussions to either of us. Tom found out through some other sources in the plant that the main focus of suspicion was on some other "innocent" drug dealer in the assembly area on the second shift. It was suspected that A turned in B to take over his area. That was probably Tom's original plan, but things don't always turn out the way you plan. One of my brothers once told me that over 95 percent of everyone he knew was working on, at least, "plan B" by now in their lives. Sort of a sobering thought, isn't it?

In Tom's case, things went wrong on the outside with some stolen credit cards and who was making what profit off the caper, and things got too hot for him to come to work for about a week or so. Missing three days of work, with no prior notice, constitutes a "voluntary quit" by the shop rules, and he knew he had a problem with me, as I would not overlook the incident and take him back. His parole officer knew what was going on, at least as far as work was concerned, and was looking for Tom, too. If the parole officer had found him, he would have had to stand in line to do anything about it; trust me. Tom called me and asked what

73

I was going to do about it. I told him that as far as I was concerned, he had quit, and if he wanted to come back, he would have to go through other channels than me. Meaning I wasn't going to take him back under any circumstances and he would have to find another sucker. I did tell him it was nothing personal, I liked him, and he had always done a good job for me. If he could convince me that he had cleaned up his act of selling and using, I would be happy to have him back. We both knew that was not going to happen. Certainly not while we were talking on the phone or in the near future, for that matter. I never heard from him again, but I did receive one phone call from the plant doctor, who, if you will remember earlier, had told us that we had no drug problem in the plant whatsoever. Of course not. If you needed or wanted drugs, you could get them anywhere, no problem. He called and asked me to take Tom back on his old job. When I asked, "Why would I want to hire back a known drug pusher and drug user?" he told me that everybody deserved another chance. I told him if he wanted Tom back to give him a job in his office, not on my floor. That didn't seem to set too well with him, and I further reinforced it by telling him that if I ever saw or heard of Tom being taken back from the voluntary quit over my protestations, he could be looking for a job, too. I don't know what I would have been able to do about it, but I surely would have made a heck of a lot of noise about it. It must have worked, as that was the last I ever heard of the incident one way or the other. Thank God.

Well, that was one part of it. The next part was even more bizarre. That's the part where I fired the undercover agent because no one told me who he was, as they weren't sure I could be trusted!

10

Rock-'n'-Roll

by Les Wheeler

After firing the undercover agent, who, I might say, surely had it coming, I was not the favorite son in the area. It wasn't that I had done the wrong thing; it was that I made the "big guys" look nearly as stupid as they really were. Had they the sense to tell me or my boss about this big drug dealer, as we were responsible for his ultimate ouster, their "plant" might have stayed on and gotten a few more. Part of the problem was that a lowly supervisor had known about the bust and they didn't have any part in it, because we didn't tell them. Partly because of my source and partly because we weren't sure they could be trusted. After all, they were letting the dealer operate, with their permission, while the sting was going on. So, in retaliation and hoping to grab some glory of their own, they planted one in my department and "neglected" to tell me. When the guy came into my area, he assumed I knew and he acted like it was OK to do whatever he wanted to do. I would let him do nothing as long as he made contacts with known drug dealers in the area. Had I known, I might have let him do what he was doing and tried to cover his path with my regular employees. But, since I had no knowledge of what was going on, I was left with no choice, at least in my eyes. Should I keep an employee who had not gained

seniority and didn't look like he was going to be a good employee, or should I ditch the sucker and dip back into the hiring
pool and take my chances on the next one? Hey, no contest, the
deadbeat had to go before he attained seniority and became that
much harder to get rid of. That's the kind of decision that's easy
to make—bye-bye, baby!

I wish that was the end of the drug stories. It isn't. I had
one more guy in the area who was making it increasingly difficult
for me. I could never catch him actually pushing the stuff on
anyone, but I was sure he was and rumors from the other guys,
in the area, sort of confirmed it for me. Some of the symptoms
of the disease are: carrying a briefcase to and from the rest room
any time you went, carrying the briefcase to and from lunch and
breaks, and never having lunch in the area with the other guys
(especially if you used to). Let's just say I had my suspicions but
couldn't take them to court. I had no hard evidence to support
them. I had talked with the guy, more than once, to let him
know that I had the suspicions, without being too specific, as you
couldn't just walk up to someone and announce that you were
sure he was a drug dealer, without any proof. A bit tacky, to say
the least, as he could then call the union and get them all over
your ass for harassment and whatever they could think of next.
One good way to get the union guy on your side was to provide
him with free samples of the product. Sort of like buying insur-
ance for the future, in case you needed it. It worked.

Some days you get up in the morning wondering if this is
the right job for you, or any sane person, for that matter. You
might even wonder if there was a God and why he would let this
go on. And then, from out of the blue, from out of nowhere or
a completely unexpected source comes the answer you were hoping for. There is a God, and he was in your corner.

I was in my department, completing some paperwork, when
a friend of mine, Donny (a fictitious name) from the safety department, came by and asked if he could buy me a coffee. Now,

hardly anyone comes from the front of the complex to the back to buy you a coffee unless they want something from you. Especially if the temperature happens to be in the nineties and they have to leave their air-conditioned office to buy you this coffee. Hard to believe, so I didn't. I knew Donny wanted something from me, but I couldn't figure out what it was. My mind was racing as I tried to guess in my mind what was on his mind and prepare my defense before he popped the question at me. I reasoned that a good defense was the best offense in this case. So I was very unprepared for what was really on his mind as we were buying the coffee from the nearest machine. As we were walking back to my desk, he asked if we could drink the coffee in my boss's office area, as it was decidedly cooler in there. Not being a total idiot, although some people, including Rino, might dispute that, I agreed. I figured that whatever Donny wanted to do to me, it would probably feel better if I was at least somewhat cool. Little did I know, at the time, that his news would have been welcome if I had to get it standing in a pizza oven on a hot day. Anyway, I was ready for whatever he had to give.

His first question was if "so and so" worked for me. Now I knew that Donny knew the answer before he asked me or he wouldn't have bought me the coffee in the first place and I would be outside sweating at my desk. Well, two can play that game, so I said, "He might. Why?" Donny then asked if he was a good employee or what. Now my suspicions were up. No one asked that kind of question unless he had something on the guy and wanted to know if you would pursue it before he made a big stink of it. This was a good, safe practice to follow, as some supervisors would not follow up on a murder charge if it involved some type of discipline to one of their favorite employees. I would guess that Donny had been burnt once or twice before and wasn't going to be burnt again, if he could help it. I didn't blame him for being cautious, but I could hardly wait to hear what it was he had on my guy, and visions of dire things, which would hold dire consequences, danced through my head. I told him that the guy was a suspected drug dealer and not a premium employee, by any means, even if I didn't have those suspicions. What did Donny have in mind? He then proceeded to tell me one of the most bizarre stories I had ever heard.

Donny related to me that my guy and someone else who worked in the safety department as a clerk had been stealing company property, at a pretty fair clip, for some time now. In those days, we didn't have computers to keep track of anything and for identification purposes all we had were badges that were made up by the safety department clerk. The clerk was supplying my guy with phony badges, and then my guy would purchase items from the safety department without ever having to pay for them. Sort of a neat idea when you think about it, but the killer here is, What can you buy from the safety department that is worth losing your job over? Not much. The shoe store, located in the safety department stocked a good number of safety shoes, the steel-tipped kind, and assorted socks and what have you. The shoes were top quality and at a fair price for the workers already, so buying them with phony identification to sell them anywhere would not make you rich for a long, long time, if ever. It seems as if the boys were finally caught by Donny after an inventory showed a number of shortages that were not paid for. It's kind of tough to payroll-deduct any amount from someone who doesn't even exist, let alone work here. The only real proof we had was the purchase of twelve pairs of work socks. Twelve lousy pair of socks could possibly cost both of them their jobs and perhaps hinder them from future employment at General Motors. Not a good deal.

That was the crux of the charge: misappropriation of company property, a dischargeable offense, and Donny wondered if my guy was bad enough for me to push the issue. No problem, he was going to take a hard fall if I even thought we could make it stick. Remember that I was sure he was a drug pusher and he wasn't a good worker anyway. Not that I ever put this kind of an issue up to a vote, but if I was to survey the rest of the department and tally up the votes, my guy would have been out in a New York minute. In any department where you have to work as a team, if one guy is not pulling his own weight, the other guys will do one of two things: get into his shit and get him to do his share or, if that doesn't work, go to the supervisor with their complaints and hope that he will do something to get rid of the guy. They tried number one and it didn't work, so they were pretty open to the next step. They didn't have to take the next step. Donny showed up with the good news first.

I had a brief consultation with my immediate supervisor (of all the supervisors I've worked for, this particular supervisor was either the best or tied for the top), who approved our next move, which would be a disciplinary interview with my guy, then a decision on what to do next, based on that interview. In some cases and with some supervisors, they had the paperwork typed and in their pocket before they even told the employee that the interview was going to be held—sort of a guilty verdict before they heard all the evidence or, for that matter, any of the evidence. It's kind of a funny approach, as you have to make certain that you have some kind of a case before you take that step, but you don't want to prejudice the outcome before you make too many moves. Sometimes when you had a good case against somebody, especially a bad-assed dude you really wanted out, you took more precautions, ahead of time, to avoid any problems later, but it was worth the effort in the long run. I was sure I could make it stick and that, from my experience, I had enough of a case to go for it. But standards must be maintained even when you were so hot to get the guy that you were dangerously close to an orgasm of monumental proportions.

I called my guy over to my desk and informed him that I had some information about him that might lead to his being disciplined later and would like to hold a disciplinary interview with him now. At this time, I advised him of his right to have a committeeman present, if he so wished. An interesting point here is that many of the employees felt that requesting to have their committeeman present was an admission of guilt and usually didn't ask for him to be there. Fine by me, but you had to advise them anyway.

I took due care not to tell him of the gravity of the charge, only that a charge of some sort was possibly going to be made. Generally, crooks inside are just like crooks outside: they never think they are going to be caught and still don't think they are caught even when shown the evidence. He agreed to the interview, without the representation, and we went into my boss's office. It was also generally accepted that you didn't try to pull off an interview on the floor in your department, because of the possible embarrassment for you and or the employee. These interviews had also been known to explode into violence when the accused realized that his shit was bad and you could prove it beyond a doubt. Given the fact that I was sure he was a drug dealer and had a gun on his person, I was not too thrilled about being alone in an office with him for any length of time. Naturally, he brought into the office with him his briefcase, which was, of course, where I was sure the gun was. As in real life, you couldn't just call up the local police and tell them to search this guy's briefcase unless you had seen the weapon or had a hot tip. I suppose I could have lied about it, but that thought never occurred to me. I don't mind playing hardball, but it's going to be a level field, from my end of the court anyway.

One other little item I almost forgot to tell you was that we also used Blue Cross cards as a form of identification in the old days, because everyone had one and they were supposed to be one of a kind for each employee. As we later found out, the clerk in the safety department could make them up with a little help from someone he knew who was working in a hospital. Well, that's another story and leads me astray from this one, but the spiral never seemed to end and just picked up speed as it went sucking even more people than we had ever thought it could. Before it was all over, three months later, several more employees, both hourly and salaried, were implicated and subsequently discharged. In this instance, I was not aware of my guy having the incriminating card on him as I wasn't aware of its existence. The card itself only became important when my guy tried to dispose of it later.

We sat down in the office, with an air of trepidation on my part, and we both could feel the tension. He knew, from my reputation, that I wouldn't be doing this unless I had something, but I think he thought that it was only a bluff on my part concerning his activities with drugs and he was pretty sure I couldn't prove anything in that area. So, he must have figured that he could beat the rap. However, as soon as I started to query him about his association with the clerk in the safety department, he started to get that squirmy feeling in his pants, like I had dropped some fire ants down his drawers. His eyes opened wider and they started to dart about the room like he was expecting the other shoe to drop any second and was looking for a quick way out of the room. Not to disappoint him, I dropped the other shoe in his lap. I asked him if he had made any purchases, of anything, from the safety department shoe store recently. I glanced down at my notes and paused to heighten the moment, and in the blink of an eye he leaped up and bolted from the office. Of course, he took his briefcase with him as he made his run for the door. Unfortunately, we had not really planned on this happening and hadn't taken any precautions to stop it. Also, unfortunately, this particular office setup had a front and back door. Not a good deal for me. At the time, it seemed like I had no choice but to follow him out the door, whether I thought he had a gun on him or not. Rino was to later remind me, many times, how stupid that move was and how dangerous the next moves I made were. I wasn't born stupid, but if shit went bad here, I was certainly going to die stupid.

I jumped up from the desk, yelled to my immediate supervisor and Donny that the guy had beaten the scene, and was out the back door. I told them to call Plant Protection, give them the details, including my suspicion of the weapon (which, in retrospect, was to prove to be my second straight stupid move in less than one minute), and the direction we were taking as I went out the back door after my guy. I caught up with him in the aisle heading west toward the back entrance and exit of the plant. He was heading at a pretty good clip at the time. We weren't running, but we weren't walking either. It was a pace that could best be described as Olympic or power walking. I'm sure you get the picture. I asked him where he was going, and he told me that he had to take a leak. I told him that was OK, but did we have to walk so fast to get there? He took a sudden left-hand turn up the escalator to the upstairs cafeteria without answering me and started to take the steps two or three at a time to get to the top. I guess he thought that if he made the men's rest room before I got there, he could ditch what I was sure was a weapon he didn't want to have on him when we processed him out. I was just as determined that I wasn't going to let him out of my sight long enough to flush anything down the drain, be it drugs or the gun. So, up the stairs I went right on his butt all the way. We both made the door to the rest room at practically the same moment, and since this was a small rest room, he could see that there was no way to dispose of anything without me seeing it. He turned around quickly enough to almost knock me down and went back out the door we had just came in.

Again, I'm assuming that he was trying to lose me, as he took off down the escalator, not the steps, dodging most everyone coming up the escalator at the time. Seeing that he would have more problems on the escalator than I would on the steps, I took the steps two or three at a time on the way down, which is no mean trick, let me tell you: I was able to reach the bottom before him. When he got to the bottom he saw me and, to my surprise, took a right-hand turn heading back to where we had started. Again, I got alongside of him and questioned him as to his intent. Where were we going and why? Did he realize that this was not making the situation any better? He again told me that he had to take a leak and headed for the nearest rest room. This rest room just happened to be right next to my department and just outside of the office that we had originally left. As we were headed down the aisle, I contemplated my good fortune as I realized where we were now headed. Again, a clear example of stupidity feeding upon itself. I think I had not yet figured out what I was going to do, whenever we got to wherever we were going. Luckily, when the opportunity presented itself, I didn't think but reacted and, as you will note, that's good, because no real thinking person would have thought of doing what I was going to do in the next few minutes, especially to someone he suspected of carrying a piece.

Well, we ducked into the rest room, and as I think back over this incident, it surprises me that there seemed to be no one else around while this was going on. It was almost as if we were acting out our little scenario on a sound stage, like a dress rehearsal, and no one else bothered to give us a second glance, much less realize the drama unfolding around him. As I look back, I wonder if it was the panic that must have been exuding from every pore of my body and, for that matter, his body, too. Whatever, no one seemed to notice or to care. Perhaps it was that they noticed and consciously decided not to notice? The old "I don't want to get involved" syndrome?

Whatever, there we were and my guy got there first, ducked into the first stall, shut the door, and latched it behind him. Believe it or not, my reaction was to say to myself, knowing that I was lying (what a lowlife, lying to yourself in times of stress!), *He said he had to take a leak; that doesn't require a stall with the door shut.* So, not knowing what else to do, I gathered my strength and kicked the door off its hinges. Needless to say, it surprised him as much as it did me. This was another of those fine points that Rino would point out to me for years to come (he still does), that it was probably the single most stupid act I had ever pulled in my life, and, if there is indeed reincarnation after death, probably the single most act of stupidity in my next two lives also. The look of astonishment on my guy's face almost made me laugh. If I hadn't been so keyed up by the whole thing, I might have laughed, but it wasn't funny for about six beers after the whole thing was over far later in the night. To conclude, the guy didn't have a gun or dope or a job. We ended our walk at the personnel office where he was processed out the door never to be heard from again.

As you may have noticed by now, we had covered a great deal of real estate and used up a good amount of time without seeing anyone from plant protection. It was my decided unluck that "Sir Chicken Little" was on the horn when my call came in informing them that I was in the building, chasing a suspected armed employee, and needed help. Guess which building they looked in for us? You got it. They were looking everywhere we weren't, in hopes of not finding us until they could be sure I had disarmed him or he was out of ammunition, which, in my case, would probably have been the worst-case scenario for me, to say the least.

11

Dead Horses Ride Again

by Les Wheeler

You would think that dead horses would go away and become part of the nearest glue factory, but it doesn't always happen that way. Some of the bosses we have had over the years should have been put out to pasture long before they were, and some are still working even though their usefulness has long since passed. Some of the real workhorses have been put out to the glue factory because they didn't "measure" up to the good old boy's ideas of the right thing to do. It is certainly not a case of whether or not you have the right stuff. It's a question of whether or not you will knuckle under and sell your soul for the privilege of being a member of the crowd. I really wonder if it was ever worth it for those who did sell themselves so short, or were they just so shallow that they never even noticed that they had, in fact, sold their integrity to be one of the guys that has lost General Motors a significant amount of market share?

There was a television commercial on that showed a top executive of an unknown automobile company chewing out his executives for loss of sales. One executive decides to stand up to him and suggests to him that they should start building quality into their cars, like the car manufacturers they were losing sales to. The last scene you see is the older executive asking, "Are there any more questions?'' as the camera pans his captive audience and shows us an ''empty'' seat. Obviously, the executive is gone. This has happened and still happens, not only in General Motors and the automobile industry, but also in our government, where we have the ''1959'' style of management that still goes on. The only way they go away is when they retire. The new management is thankful and throws a lavish retirement party, but in the back of their minds they know they can now get on with getting the business in the direction it should be going in.

We went through this same experience portrayed in the TV commercial at the GM Building on the seventh floor. They gave one of their chief executives a fine retirement in May of 1994, said all the right things, and would continue to pay him a hefty retirement check. I'll guarantee you that they, the new top executives, were also saying, ''Now that he's gone, let's get down to business!''

There was another character that had the habit of coming into my office and plopping himself into my only extra chair, putting his feet up on my desk space, and launching into some rambling fishing or hunting story that I had probably heard three times already, but I knew he was going to be there for the duration or even longer unless I could get rid of him. Shooting him was out of the question, as there were too many witnesses and even if most of them wouldn't say a word about seeing it, the mess would be too much to clean up. One thing we did have going for us was that he was pretty much of an asshole to everyone, so the other guys and I looked out for each other in situations like this. A little background here. His wife worked not very far away. She would call him at least ten times a day, and God forbid if he didn't answer the phone, for any reason, when she called. We all knew this and if he happened to trap one of us in our office, the rest of us had a pact that we would take whatever measures necessary to get him out of there. When he was there, it didn't matter if you had ten thousand things to do, places to go, or people to see to get your job done, he was there until you died or he got tired of telling you stories you had already heard and didn't want to hear the first time, let alone the second or third or fourth time.

One of our best ploys was to play on his fear of his wife. One of the most fortunate supervisors (anyone who didn't have this guy in his office at the moment) would call his office and let the phone ring. If he didn't hear it, the unfortunate one who was trapped would look up and say, "Is that your phone?" The look of consternation that would come over his face made it worth it. He was worried that she would hang up before he could answer it and then who knew what might happen? Off he would go to try to get there before that happened. The trick was to let it ring until he opened the door of his office and then hang up. Great fun for the audience. Everyone else in the area knew what was going on and enjoyed this treat, perhaps because he treated everyone equally poorly, although he did have a few favorites he treated worse than the rest of us. Sometimes you were in the barrel and sometimes you were outside watching, and everyone had a turn in the barrel at one time or another. This was more fun than you might imagine, because he would have to stay in the office for at least fifteen minutes in case she called back. She had, on at least one occasion, left her job to drive over to our plant to rip into him for not being there when she called. Which, when you think about it, is quite pathetic that she would think he didn't have anything else to do but wait for her calls. Like maybe he could do his job or some weird thing like that. A sorry state of affairs for all involved. The reason I know of the one instance is that all of the supervisors were in his office being collectively chewed out for some petty problem, and when the phone rang he didn't answer it. Well, next thing we know, she's in the office yelling at him, like you wouldn't yell at a dog, right in front of all of us and showing no signs of letting up soon either. So, being good guys, we all got up and kind of slid out of his office, as unobtrusively as we could, as none of us wanted her to stop. Not that we didn't feel sorry for him ('cause we didn't), but she got us out of the situation and we were quite confident that by the time she was through with him, he would have forgotten all about us and we were in the clear for at least two or three days. Past practice dictated that he couldn't leave the office for that long for fear of missing a phone call and, of course, he always had us calling and hanging up just in case he ventured out. So, it was kind of a rock-and-a-hard-place situation for him. To be sure, he had it coming for the misery he gave us; we couldn't do enough for him (or was that *to* him?) during the course of the shift.

Lest you even start to feel a glimmer of sadness for this guy, let me add a couple more things to the story line. One week he called me into his office and proceeded to chew me out something terrible for not reaching the efficiency goals for the last week. I could not figure out where he was coming from on this one. If there was one thing I prided myself on, it was reaching the goals. That was the numbers game that I played in those days, too. It kept most everyone off your back if you made efficiency for the week. A short-term goal, if there ever was one. You didn't worry about next week until next week. You never worried about next month until next month. Good marks in planning usually meant that you did everything right. That was real planning for a lot of them. So the game was played week by week, with no allowance to your year-to-date or month-to-date figures. If they could have figured out a way to do it daily, they would have. Well, there I was getting chewed on for not making efficiency when I knew that I had. You could usually calculate your efficiency to the hour, if you were any good at all, and I knew I had not made any mistakes last week. The only thing that could have gone wrong was that a pay ticket that I didn't know about, from some previous week, could have gone through and I might have been over, but never, I mean NEVER, under. You have to understand that not seeing the boss was predicated on making your efficiency. If you made it, you were fairly well assured of only seeing him on reasonably friendly terms and not having him living in your office until you straightened out this problem once and for all or, at least, until the next time it happened. Let me tell you that the prize was worth the effort. Not seeing him was enough to make any sensible supervisor run the machines himself to reach efficiency. You don't have a lot of choice here, folks; you had to stand there and take it until you could find out what the heck happened and then try to come back later and put some water on the fire. Didn't always work, but you always tried. Remember the prize!

I finally got the numbers from him, and they *were* low. I tried to figure out the problem and, for just an instant, thought that maybe I did make a mistake. After all, I was running my three departments and covering two more for my partner (who had made several life saving calls for me) who was on vacation, plus running the four departments upstairs for the supervisor who was on sick leave (tension problems due to the boss), and just maybe I had forgotten something in the heat of the night? Naw, no way. Adding up all the departments, I had approximately 110 people working for me that week. With no help from the boss, in case something went wrong, I got all the blame, and if everything went well, you guessed it: he had helped me a lot. The paperwork alone took up most of the morning if nothing went wrong. Passing out checks took most of Friday morning, and that was the day you shipped off your final tickets for the week. And that's where I made my big mistake. I was a little busy and made the fatal error of trusting the boss with the pay tickets I needed to make it for the week in one department. All he had to do was take the tickets to the clerk upstairs, lay them on the desk, and go home. Well, that turned out to be too much for him. I figured it out later that he had bumped into an old fishing buddy and they started to try to outlie each other on the one that got away.

And as he couldn't demonstrate just how big the fish was while holding the tickets, he laid them down on the nearest machine table. I suppose it would have been asking too much to expect him to pick up the tickets and take them to the clerk after all the fishing excitement, and it was. When I found out the cause of my inefficiency, I was faced with the dilemma of whether to tell him that it was his stupidity (or perhaps it really was mine for trusting him in the first place) that caused the problem or let it slide, take the heat, and look like a hero next week as I pulled the department out of the throes of one week of low efficiency. I took the easy way out and let it slide. I figured he wouldn't believe it anyway and it was easier. It was also an ace in the hole I could use one day later if I needed it. He must have known he had something to do with it or felt guilty about letting me run seven or so departments with no help from him and kind of left me alone the next week. But he was certainly there to tell me how much he knew I could do if I had the right kind of encouragement (read ass chewing here), and he might just come out and yell at me every day to help me along. What a guy, huh?

12

Times Are Changing

by Rino Pagnucco

One day while the assembly line was done, the first-line supervisors were told to attend a classroom session on "the new way of managing." It really wasn't anything new for us; we had been through these kinds of sessions many times before. When those sessions were over we were always told, "OK, that was a real nice break; now go back to business as usual." This one was different. Now, as I look back, I see this was the beginning of the change in our way of managing the business. It only took about an hour for the instructor, who was from CPC (Chevrolet Pontiac of Canada) headquarters in Warren, Michigan, to have all of us so infuriated that when we took a break we went to our supervisors and told them we weren't going back. What the instructor told us was that the first-line supervisors were the cause of the deterioration in General Motors and the loss of market share to the Japanese and the other foreign car manufacturers. We could not believe what he was saying. Instead of saying we're in a new time and that it's time to change and here are some of the ways we are going to have to change, etc., oh noooo . . . what he was saying to us was that we, the first-line supervisors, were to blame for everything that ever went wrong in General Motors, especially the poor productivity and all the quality problems. Needless to say, he sure got our attention. You can't tell me that our higher management didn't know what he was going to say; this was a setup from the word *go*. We had wondered why none of our supervisors was at the meeting. They knew damn well what was going to happen. Then they had the audacity to act surprised when we approached them on the issue. We could see that we were being set up for some unknown restructuring process and our bosses were now starting to play both ends of the field. Well, every meeting and every class session from then on was patterned around that same scenario. All of a sudden higher management told us, "We don't need you anymore, and we certainly don't need your way of thinking!" You can imagine what our reaction was to this. We came back and collectively questioned, "Wait a minute here. One day out of the clear blue you walk in and say we are the problem in all of General Motors, and that we are the people that made it go bad, and because we didn't do our job General Motors and the entire American automobile industry are going down the sewer! Why is this our fault?"

I kept saying to myself, *I did everything you, as higher management, told me to do. You even, at times, said I did very well. It was called appraisal. Why, at times, I did so well at my job, I not only got good appraisals; I also got raises and promotions along with them.* (Must have been a mistake in the system!) From 1969 to 1990, I was sent to twenty-three career development courses. They were courses ranging from presupervisor classes to problem solving and prevention to professional supervisor to statistical quality control to problem solving to new supervisor of hourly to appraisal workshops to resolving employee concerns to sexual harassment and received many recognition awards, including one from the Dale Carnegie courses.

Now all of a sudden you tell me we first-line supervisors are so screwed up that we are the cause of the problem. For heaven's sake, we wouldn't want anybody to think we could be part of the "solution" to the problem and, believe me, no one did think that! Higher management was just starting to "play" with the "new rules." These new rules were made up by higher middle management; let's call these people eighth levels. (Eighth-level managers in General Motors were called superintendents in the manufacturing areas. At Ford Motor Company and at Chrysler these levels were different numbers, but the superintendent position was always the same.) They were given open reign to make the new set of rules, and if they didn't work, well, just make some new ones, and don't forget to keep blaming those first-line supervisors for screwing up those new rules that didn't work. We were told we couldn't accept changes. At this same time, the hourly workforce could do no wrong. Our higher management and the higher management of the unions were making deals because this was the way the Japanese were doing it; this was the beginning of "team concept."

Team concept. If you were to ask the people in the plants today, "What is team concept?" I would give good odds and bet a lot of money that you wouldn't get the same answer twice. It isn't just a saying; it's about working together. It's about "every-one," and I mean everyone, achieving the same goal together. It's about everyone from the sweeper to the plant manager working, playing, and thinking together. In a sense, it really is a marriage. No one can be left out.

Unfortunately, at the Romulus plant they wanted to go in this direction so fast that they couldn't see the trees through the forest in many of their decisions. You know, they were getting pressure from downtown: get the system in place no matter what! So they did. "No matter what" really meant they could do any-thing. They were in charge. They could make and change the rules any time they wanted, and believe me, they did. They started teaching in two places, themselves and also the hourly. Well, what happened to the people in the middle? The supervisors? The people below us were getting trained; the people above us were getting trained; what about the first-line supervisors? You know, the ones that had to carry out the orders. You see, higher management still maintained the old practice of "production first." "We need them now, but only for a little while, until we get things in place." This was a perfect time for those eighth-level managers to pit the hourly people "against" the first-line supervisors. In a sense, they were telling the hourly people, "This is your chance to get rid of those idiots that you always wanted to get even with." The managers were playing "mind games" with everyone. They would make insinuations to the hourly that this was the time that they could show management that they didn't need supervisors and could make production without them. So while they trained everyone else, they used these supervisors to run the machining and production lines. Since they knew the lines the best, they could train the low-seniority employees while the higher ones went to training. I mean why send the lower-seniority employees to Team Concept? They were going to get laid off anyway, and if you had to send these employees to Team Concept they could go last. Besides, there still were these supervisors management could blame when things went wrong, and under these circumstances, whatever could go wrong did go wrong.

As long as it wasn't urgent to make production, plants could go along with the programs set up by the new way of doing business. Team meetings, quality meetings, preventative maintenance, etc. . . . there were programs for programs. It appeared that everybody and everything was involved in some sort of program. Everybody except the first-line supervisors. There was no time for them; besides, who would take their place? All of a sudden, the light comes on. Holy shit and cowabunga, now I know who is going to take my place. THE TEAM, THE FUCKING TEAM! Now you're telling me the same people you guys said were assholes yesterday are OK today and we are going to let them run the production lines. SURE . . . RRIIGGHHTT. The first-line supervisors, at first, were threatened with their job security. If this worked, they eventually wouldn't have a job. Have no fear; who would higher management blame when things went wrong? Certainly not the hourly, man; we're talking about the "UNION." Remember those people that our higher management made a deal with? Yeah, those guys. I'll say one thing about the union: they stuck together. When their chairman said something was going to happen, it happened. They may have not all agreed with it, but they stood by him. That didn't happen in management. Between the "DOERS" and the "SUCKASSES" and the ones that were in fear of reprisals, it looked like the NFL strike of the eighties. We didn't know whom to trust at any given time. Well, back to letting the "TEAM" run the business.

Higher management tried team concept at first, but they were going too fast; they didn't give any time to adjust. They weren't letting all the programs work out the bugs. They just had the programs in place, forgetting that the Japanese had years to perfect the system. Or better yet . . . Saturn. Why was team concept working so well at the Saturn plant in Spring Hill, Tennessee, right here, in the good old US of A? They didn't even try to find out what went wrong; they just looked and said, "Well, there they are; why isn't it working? Hey, hey . . . BRING BACK THOSE SUPERVISORS. Who are you going to blame? Supervisors, that's who." One thing higher management forgot. Japan or Tokyo isn't America or Romulus, and America or Romulus isn't Japan or Tokyo. They are two different places with two different lifestyles.

If something came up where all of a sudden we needed more production, then we had to somehow "put the programs on hold" or at least ease up on them until we got this "HOT" production out of the way. Time was now of the essence. We needed every piece of production that we could get our hands on. Everything now changed, but just until we didn't need that "HOT" production anymore. Then we would resume "THOSE" programs. Not that we ever stopped them; we just slowed them down a little. Now we needed the production, so what changes? Well, what was "scrap" yesterday isn't scrap anymore. We just camouflaged the process with acceptance letters that didn't really mean anything and were signed by people who also didn't mean anything, because the people that were signing them were the people that had control of the "rules." If you were to disagree with these people or wanted to know why they were changing the rules, you were slated as being a troublemaker or "NOT A TEAM PLAYER."

Here's an example. I was the supervisor of the crankshaft machining line. This line was set up with very strict blueprint specifications. I truly believe that the cranks that did make it through this high-tech production process were the best-made crankshafts produced in the country. The specifications, at this plant, were almost too tight. These were almost perfect cranks. But scrap was high because of the restrictions. Instead of doing the right thing and getting an OK from the chief engineer to do the proper testing, either in-house or at a certified testing facility, to prove your findings, it was easier to make up a letter stating: "We will put these cranks in engines and we will keep track of them." It won't hurt anything. It's "OK"; see, I have a letter saying it's "OK." The chief engineer would never sign his name on any of these letters. He would always say, "Do the proper testing and give me the test results." If they turned out well, he would suggest changing the specifications. It would help lower the scrap rate and still would be producing a very good part. This letter was signed by a superintendent, a general foreman, and the day shift supervisor, who was deeply intimidated by all these people. If that wasn't enough, they told the day shift supervisor to put out a new letter stating that they would be the only shift to recheck the scrap, plus we were not to put scrap cranks into the scrap tubs anymore. We were to "neatly and gently" put them onto skids. (I wonder why?)

You can see how "TEAM CONCEPT" was working here, or should I say wasn't working? The day shift could recheck the cranks, just in case there really wasn't anything wrong with them. You never know ... those gauges were probably "LYING"; they just weren't "LYING" when they made all those good ones. Hey, we got this letter now, hot off the Xerox machine. Let's cut out the bullshit; remember, time is of the essence. Those cranks that were not to specification yesterday, they're OK now? This really only happened when a machine broke down and there weren't enough crankshafts for the assembly line to run, and yes indeed, you guessed it, and try to make production if they could, which was very seldom done anyway on straight time. Don't forget it's OK now; we have this letter.

Well, one day after we had a team meeting on the second shift, the team wanted to know what the hell this letter that everyone in the assembly area was talking about was. Also, why wasn't the second shift allowed to recheck the scrap cranks? One more question: why were we using the "customer" as the "sample" of this last test? There I go again ... not a team player. One of the questions that was brought up to me at this time was: "Why can't you shut up and just do your job?" *Silly me*, I thought. Quality was part of not only my job, but everybody's job. Just what was my fucking job, to do whatever higher management wanted even if it was wrong? Not today, asshole!

At this time, the team and I weren't satisfied with the answers that were given to us. We had only one route to go, and that was to get the plant quality representatives. They would have the final say. They were made up by one representative from the union and one representative from management. The chief engineer—remember, who "wouldn't" sign that so-called letter of acceptance—would not get involved because management politics were now involved. He stated that his job was to design the product, not manage the business. Getting back to the two quality representatives, usually they were very good at what they did and were very thorough in their decision making process. You might say they were like "umpires." So you know this was not a good situation to be in. Higher management did not want them in your department, because it usually meant that there was a quality problem that was going unresolved. Even the "team" couldn't resolve it. This meant that everyone, from the plant manager to the sweeper, now knew your department had a problem, and the worst thing that could possibly happen to a manufacturing department or an assembly line was about to happen. When these two people came into your area and the team came together to find out the decision, production stopped. This type of visibility was not good in the eyes of higher management. You see, now you not only couldn't handle the situation, but you also didn't know how to "bullshit" your way through it convincingly. Remember, "the first liar wins." Did I say lie? Maybe what I really meant was to exaggerate the truth.

Well, the lead general foreman and the two quality representatives came to a special team meeting to discuss the problems that we had. The lead general foreman came in place of the superintendent of machining. This particular superintendent didn't like this type of adversity, so he almost always sent this one particular general foreman to handle the problems. In this case, this general foreman was short, grossly overweight, and smoking a cigarette whenever we saw him. But unmistakably he was the most "intimidating" and, by far, the best "bullshitter" in the land. They started to tell us that we didn't have the necessary help, meaning a full-time process engineer like the day shift had, to disconnect the proper parameters on the Marpose final inspection gauge, which would eliminate some of the specifications that would "now" make these questionable bad parts good. The "rule" was that only the departmental process engineer could tamper or change the parameters of that gauge. So when the day shift reran the suspected out-of-tolerance cranks, which normally were scrap, they now would be OK. Wait a fucking minute here; we had those specifications and parameters in place, because they're on the blueprint. In order to take them off the blueprint or change the parameters for a customer's engine, we had to run many, many, many tests and show Engineering that we didn't need to be that stringent.

Well, the question was, Were we going to do the sampling and how were we going to get the results? The answer that was given to us was from the dealers. Yes, the car dealers. So big-mouth Rino asked a simple little question. "Does this mean from Warranty Claims?" You should have seen the look that I got from this lead general foreman. He immediately said, "No," and quickly went on to another subject. The only way a dealer could give results like that would be through excessive customer complaints and bad warranty trends. Now don't forget, we were talking to the most intimidating and the best bullshitter in the land.

Well, what about this letter everyone was talking about? They finally showed us the letter. It was a standard letter, typed by the day shift foreman, stating that we were going to use some "deviated" (or some wording to that effect) crankshafts and that we had to keep track of the serial numbers that were stamped on the engines and that made it alright to use them. There were three signatures on the letter, and it was shown to the team leaders and the supervisors on the assembly line. The three signatures were from people of no importance, because Engineering refused to sign it. We were never ever to let that letter out of our sight or give the letter to someone. The fear was that some disgruntled employee would take it to the newspapers and make an issue out of it. If I needed to show it to anyone, it would be in the day shift supervisor's top desk drawer under lock and key. Is this the way we run an honest business? You would think they were practicing working for the government! If, for one moment, you might think "I" don't have a copy of that letter, you are greatly mistaken. It's called CYA.

I really believe that most of those crankshafts were good and acceptable. It's just that they weren't the "world-class" cranks that we were used to producing. It's the "process" that

99

we were told we had to go through. If higher management had put as much time and effort into doing it the right way as they did in trying to deceive everyone, they would have had real team concept and a lot more credibility from everyone. It all revolves around the aspect and reality of "PRODUCTION FIRST!" In assembly plants throughout General Motors, except possibly Saturn, this will always, always, always be a fact of life.

One of my very good friends, Benny (a fictitious name), whom I consider one of the best supervisors of machining that I ever met, once told me what higher management considered a truly good machine shop supervisor. It all started one day when we found a problem with an engine block on the assembly line that I was running and Benny had just taken over the block line in the machine shop. I was REALLY PISSED because I wasn't going to make MY production that day, and he was REALLY PISSED because he had BEEN GIVEN this area THAT MACHINED THE ENGINE BLOCKS and it was a "junkyard" when he took it over.

Let me tell you a little about Benny. He could take an area that had gone to hell in a handbasket, that couldn't make a quality part or make production, and turn it around. If need be, he would roll up his sleeves and get right in the thick of things. His style of "getting the job done" at times was a bit archaic, but the bottom line was to get the job done, and he always did. No matter what it took, he always told it the way it was. Some people just don't like to hear that kind of talk. Management would put him in areas that couldn't make production, because he was like an "ENFORCER." They loved that style of management, but only when it was to their benefit.

Now don't get me wrong, as you read on; Benny always wanted to build a good part. But that is not what everyone wants. The bottom line is pieces. It doesn't make any difference what part you are machining. Whether it is an engine block, a camshaft, a fuel pump body, or any widget whatsoever, the theory is the same. If your people are machining the part and it goes out of blueprint specifications you, as a supervisor, must instantly know how much "out" of blueprint specifications you can go before determining whether you will have to stop making this part and be in trouble with your bosses or continue to try to get it past the final inspection station. If the part is too far out of specifications, it's junk and you can't give it to the assembly area. Needless to say, if anything is out of the blueprint specifications you should stop building or machining it.

So, at this point, you have determined that there was a problem, and you fixed the problem. But what did you do with all the pieces that are out of specifications and are now the "problem"? Here comes the theory. Here comes the challenge. Here comes the bullshit. But, nevertheless, here comes the truth. Here's what determines a good, efficient machine shop supervisor. He told me that it was his job to get those parts to the assembly line. It meant that those parts had to get approved out of his area and in and out of my area, without any repercussion. It was "my" job to find "his" mistakes. If his mistakes got by me, he did his job. He wasn't being a smartass; he was just being honest. This was absolutely devastating to me. He was, and still is, a very good friend. Here's a guy with twenty-five years' experience as a machining supervisor telling me, an assembly line supervisor of twenty-five years, what reality really was. He told me to think of it this way: What he was doing to a machined part was exactly what I was doing to an assembled engine. Once that part leaves your area; it's somebody else's problem. I could not believe I was so blind to reality. Then one day I was given a machining department.

Reality and the truth really suck. This type of reality is in the factories right now. This is what we have to change, and I believe it is changing. We must force our "management" to never go back to this kind of theory, because it is management that sets the rules, not the supervisors or the hourly people. They just do what they are told!

So what has changed in the last three decades? Schedule or production is always first; this has never changed. How we go about getting it must change. QUALITY MUST BE THE NUMBER-ONE PRIORITY. We have gotten better at buying machinery and assembly lines that have high-tech quality features already built into them. These built-in features should almost never be tampered with, and if they are it should only be for improvement in the quality of the product.

When I first became a supervisor, back in 1969, I was taught this simple rule: If you improve quality first everything will fall in line. Production will increase, scrap will decrease, and your overall efficiency will be higher. That just brings me to another part of my new education. They also told us that we should "FORGET ABOUT EFFICIENCY." At this point, I damn well knew that they had lost their minds. In 1990, General Motors wrote off $700 million. Like it was nothing, this was, in fact, a normal operating procedure. They just said to themselves, "Let's start over." Don't you wish you could do that? Let's try it; just write checks for more money than you really have. When you find out you are overdrawn, just say to yourself, *Gee, I guess that was a bad decision. Oh well, we'll just start over*. This type of poor and bad decision making, by the very highest management in General Motors, is still going on today. They truly believe that there is no end to the money and because we are General Motors we will always recover. You see, the enormous salaries haven't stopped; the bonuses haven't stopped. The big, lavish parties, the overly expensive hotel stays (like at the Victorian in Phoenix, Arizona), and the excessive spending by all divisions haven't stopped. Well, let me tell you, the loss of jobs hasn't stopped, and the loss of market share hasn't stopped either. Since 1990,

General Motors has lost over $16.9 billion. *B* for *billion*, let there be no mistake. I think, for once, they did exactly what they were told. They forgot about efficiency. Is there any wonder why the deficit in America is what it is today?

13

Intimidation 101

by Rino Pagnucco

The definition, in my opinion, of intimidation is fucking someone else over very politely and then saying "Thank you." (Well, maybe you won't find those exact words in the dictionary, but you get the idea.) Bill Lambier, former player of the Detroit Pistons, was, in my opinion, intimidating, a police officer can be intimidating, but nobody was more intimidating than the GM managers that I had dealings with at the Romulus Engine plant in Romulus, Michigan, during the beginning of the 1982–83 revamping of General Motors.

How is intimidation related to what happens in the work force? Intimidation in the workforce could be a combination of many things, and I would be willing to bet that you can relate to these examples in your own work environment or even at home. How about this statement? "Yes, you can do it your way, but, you know, tomorrow you could be needed on midnights! Not because we are punishing you, but because we need you and your experience there. We think it will be good for you and your career and, of course, it would also be good for the company." What a crock of shit that was, but I bet you've heard something like this sometime in your career. See, the problem with my partner and me was that we wouldn't bow to these demands if we truly believed they were going in the wrong direction. We were also taught that in America if you are right, nothing bad should happen to you. We were also taught by our parents that if you always tell the truth you will never get in trouble. (My, how times have changed.) My partner and I have not lied about anything we have said, and we can prove everything we have said if need be. So let's just say it this way: we weren't intimidated . . . we were just fucked with a lot. I experienced that intimidating style of management until the end of 1990, when I left by transferring out of the Romulus plant. Keeping in touch with some of my sources, I know it's still practiced there now, and some say it's worse now than it has ever been, or at least at the time during which I was writing this book. (A new set of managers came in from Flint, Michigan, and were professional intimidators, only proving that some sort of intimidation is everywhere, especially where power struggles seem to be.) It was at this time I watched managers who really took advantage of their positions. The eighth levels and above, and some "kiss-ass" sixth and seventh levels. Those sixth- and seventh-level managers were just being used, only they couldn't see that when higher management was done with them, they were next on the chopping block.

You can even see, at times, the eighth levels that wanted to stay close to the unclassified people that had the real power. These eighth levels would get together with a select few of their own and gang up on one of their own or whoever it might be until that one individual had nowhere else to go but out. He would get transferred or ask to be transferred somewhere else. They would set someone up so that person would look bad in front of higher management or, even more dangerous, the union. Don't forget we were in team concept. If you made the union look bad to the people you put into positions who were supposed to work together, they would start dropping little hints to the RMS (Romulus Management System) committee. Let's see what I can compare this to. . . . Um . . . OK, how about the Third Reich? The RMS committee was all the people on the top structure of the plant: the plant manager, the head of personnel, all the people who made the rules in the first place. Don't forget, they could also change the rules whenever they wanted to. The little hints the union would drop would be statements like: "You should be thinking about making some moves."

There was really only three, at best sometimes four, eighth-level individuals who were really pretty smart—or should I say in control—and they would not let anyone else into their comfort zone. They watched out for each other. They were always looking for a larger piece of the pie. The more pie, the more power. At the drop of a hat they would turn on each other. They thrived on intimidation; the more they intimidated, the more they wanted to intimidate.

It all started with that meeting all the supervisors went to that I talked about earlier. After that all hell was about to break loose, and nobody on salary was safe from some sort of intimidation. There was a hidden clique, a small clique that had four main "screws." These screws would allow others into their little clique only to use them, and once the screws were done with them or they started to become a problem, the screws would turn on them.

Let me give you a few examples. If they needed to get rid of some head count (personnel), they would go about it in various different manners. They could go from one end of the spectrum to the other. They would, all of a sudden, make someone look like he wasn't doing a good job or promote him and then transfer him out. There was a young lady in the time study department. Out of the clear blue, she was called into her boss's office, with other members of management there, and told they didn't need her anymore. They called the security people down; they told her to clear her personal items out of her desk and leave. They told her, "Go home; we will call you." This was truly intimidation at its best. Talk about being fucked with! One minute everything is OK; the next minute you don't know what the hell hit you. You see, she wasn't fired, she wasn't laid off, she was told to go home, just go home, with pay. But "don't come back; we will call you." The idea was to screw with her mind so bad that she could not think straight, in hope that she just might quit out of frustration. Then the bottom line is . . . they won. You're off the head count and it was "YOUR" decision. During this time, you are in such a state of confusion, you don't know what to say, if anything, to family, friends, or anyone. You just want to cover your head and hide.

Then there was this personnel manager. He was let into the clique early on in the same game because they needed someone that the rest of the salary people still trusted. He was well liked and respected by just about everyone. They kept him on to take the heat and pass out the dirty work. Well, one day, we all believe, he saw the light and finally said to himself, "Hey, wait a minute; you really can't do what you're doing, in the manner in which you are doing it, to these people." We could see he was starting to answer back. Well, it didn't take long until they were done "using" him. Couldn't use this fool anymore, so they "PRO-MOTED" him. He went on to the GM Building in downtown Detroit. Well, isn't that special! They just neatly got rid of him.

Then there was the guy who was in charge of training. Same thing. Took him in, made him part of the clique, and commenced to use him. They started to redirect his thinking and even made him say some things that he knew weren't quite right, but because of the situation he was put in, he had to do it. He was told to set up training programs in a certain way, and when they didn't work, not because of him or his staff, they were just bad programs that he was given, or some union guy got his feathers bent out of shape. Regardless, the blame was on this guy, for doing what he was told to do. He also finally started to ask the clique questions, and lo and behold, he found himself transferred to a job at the Tech Center in Warren, Michigan. Two separate incidents caused these two to go on to "better" pastures.

There were some reasons why these things were happening.

One, the population of the plant was getting smaller. That was due to no rehires on retirements, transfers with no replacements, buyouts, etc. So now the piece of the pie, or let's call it turf, was more important than ever. See, you had the same amount of managers, but a smaller number of people to manage. On this note, General Motors basically runs the same way, all the way from the fourteenth floor at 3044 West Grand Boulevard in Detroit, Michigan, to all the little plants anywhere in the world. It basically runs the same way as the "gangs" of Los Angeles, Chicago, and Miami. It's about "TURF." Turf or the piece of the pie, same thing. In General Motors and at the Romulus plant, it was now about turf. The question became: "How can I get more turf? I need to have more people under my responsibility." Now the questions were who had a "weak" spot and who could we fuck over. Or, better yet, "Here's how we're going to do it. I can get one of the other eighth levels and kind of gang up on this poor schmuck and make him look bad from two sides of management. Then we can split his turf between us. We have now succeeded in two things. One . . . a bigger piece of the pie, which also means more turf. Two . . . we have now succeeded in intimidating one of our own."

The second incident that I just talked about was a bit unusual because it started out as the clash of the eighth levels and we could see this, but we couldn't do anything about it and we didn't want to, because as long as they were fighting among themselves we, the first-line supervisors, were safe. The training eighth-level coordinator realized what was happening and thought he could fight it—he was tight with the union, and he had some good salary backing. So what went wrong? Well, the union was making some of their own moves and the part he was tight with was not as powerful. As far as the salary backing that he had, it was only the sixth levels and below, and we were fighting to save our jobs also. Talk about bad timing. The system, the Romulus system, was against him. Next thing you know, the screws were tightened.

Some responsibilities were taken away. He was given "shit jobs," an insult to himself and his level. They even helped him find a job at the GM Tech Center in Warren. Boy, are these people wonderful or what?

These were just two situations of many that I and many others have seen happen. I could probably write another book just on the many situations created by intimidation at that plant. If you have ever been in a "management changeover," from either takeovers or down-sizing various companies into one, you know what we have been through. It's similar to a movie called *Brubaker* (1980), starring Robert Redford, where a new warden tries to make things right for the prisoners but has to fight the "system" to do so and finally gains respect from the prisoners and the staff but loses his job to the "system." This, unfortunately, happened to me and some of the people I have just talked about. (They tell me another management change has recently happened there and the "games" are continuing at a more rapid pace.) In my situation, and to my credit, if I may add, I was respected, if not liked, by all sides. I was kind of an all-around likable guy, liked by salary, liked by hourly, and somewhat liked by the union. To this day, I truly believe management found me the job I had before I took an early retirement. I miss the many friends that I left behind and thank God for the job I went into, as it restored my trust that, yes, in spite of the system, there are also places in General Motors that are trying to go in the right direction.

You see, 1982–83 was the beginning of the "changes." In 1986–87 more changes were happening, only this time more drastic changes. The changes in 1982–83 weren't enough; the red ink in General Motors was flowing even heavier. Ford Motor Company made their drastic changes in the beginning and only lost some monies for a short period of time. They were able to make improvements as they were making changes. I would also bet that during the drastic change time the intimidation factor at Fo-MoCo was at an all-time high.

During 1986–87, another meeting happened at our plant. We were told all salary people, regardless of level, were to take a test, a psychological test. We would also be required to take an oral interview in front of a panel (the clique) to find out whether we were acceptable as supervisors under the new direction that General Motors wanted to go in at this time. If not, we were going to be placed somewhere else. They wouldn't tell us where—limbo, so to speak. Now you want to talk about mental intimidation, this was it.

Now, let me get this straight. I have been a supervisor for twenty-plus years and you said I was OK, but that was yesterday. Today I have to take a psychological test and undergo an oral interview to see if I can keep my job. I am surprised that we didn't have to take a urine test. I still think the clique should have taken a urine test . . . because, in my opinion, they damn sure had to be on drugs. During the time of the testing, we had people from an outside testing company talk with us. It was kind of a question-and-answer period, only during this question-and-answer time, we all had a sneaking suspicion the interviewers were sort of "feeling us out," taking mental notes on every one of us, and returning this information to the superintendents who were making the decisions on whom they were going to keep as supervisors. I finally asked one of them what her qualifications were for giving us the test and evaluating us while we were being tested. She said she used to work for the telephone company as a supervisor for the telephone operators. I am going to leave this one alone, folks, because, to this day, I still don't know what made her qualified to give these tests and ask us questions that would determine the fate of our livelihood. A lot of people who took the test thought that, after the testing, the clique would decide who was going to continue as supervisors, but others believed the list was already made before the tests were given and this was just a camouflage procedure.

For the oral review, you were called into a room and told you were either accepted or not accepted. The ones that were not accepted . . . well, the clique would deal with them later. The ones that did make it were now put into a position of being told how to act and talk. At this point, if you were selected, you would think you would be happy, but because of all that you had been put through, there was a funny feeling and it wasn't a happy feeling. It was a feeling of relief and of bitterness. After they made their choices, you knew if they made the wrong choice, they were going to deal with you later. They were upfront and told you that, so you always had that hanging over your head. Then, when they were short of supervisors for vacation replacements or sick leaves, they went back to the same supervisors they had told were not good enough to be supervisors before and "now" told them they were good enough to fill in the open spots. Always with the understanding that they could change their minds, and send these supervisors back into their limbo state any time they wanted to. Intimidation 101, these people were at the head of their class at it. They were the best at playing the "game," that is, the proverbial "mind game."

There was another example of intimidation that involved two women. Both of these women were chosen as coordinators. One was a supervisor of hourly people before the testing, and the other was not but was very talented and well deserving of the job. So, now we have women also. Don't forget the female quota. (If you still believe that the big companies that get the big government contracts don't have minority quotas, you are not dealing with Intimidation 101 reality.) Within a year, one of the women took the buyout, basically because they wouldn't let her do anything and paid no attention to her, even though she was there. Higher management just turned their backs on her, which was another form of intimidation. Again, they went into her mind and messed with it. Higher management didn't do anything, nothing; they just stood back and acted like she wasn't even there.

They gave her simple, menial jobs, rarely followed up, and very rarely paid any attention to her. They knew what kind of a supervisor she was, that she had to be doing something all the time. Higher management knew it was important to her to be in charge and responsible for something; that was her personality. I could never understand why they "dumped" her. She was very good at her job, no matter what the job was. They won . . . she eventually quit, took the buyout, and it was "her" decision.

The other woman was, in many ways, subjected to sexual harassment situations, but because of her floor experience, she had the "street sense" not to stoop to their level of incompetence and she survived. She chose to go to another location. The bottom line was . . . she left. I understand she got a job at the Tech Center, got a well-deserved promotion, and is working with some good GM people that are going in the right direction. There was a lot of borderline sexual harassment. I mean, in some cases, higher management was the epitome of stupidity. They would send a certain group of people that worked for them to a sexual harassment class and while they were at the class, some of the "more stupid" eighth-level managers that were not attending the class would be making sexual gestures and overtures to some of the women that were still working on their jobs. These kind of games, I am sure, are played all too often, not only in corporate America, but everywhere, even at the corner store down the street. From the simplest type of intimidation to the hard-line, knock-down type of intimidation, they just didn't care who you were. They were definitely an equal opportunity employer of intimidation at this point. You could be the fourth-level clerk or an unclassified production manager. When it was "your" time to be intimidated, you were next! At one time, GM philosophy was "Our people are our greatest asset." Now it is just a statement of the past and could be put into the category of a "false and vicious rumor."

I can remember when the Romulus plant was in such a state of confusion, we had no idea who our leader was. At one point, we had: 1.) a plant manager; 2.) a manager of plant managers, whose job before this one had several plant managers reporting directly to him (he thought he was the plant manager); and, last but not least, 3.) a new production manager, who thought he was sent there to get things going and then retire the one plant manager and oust the other so he could be the plant manager. If you think this situation was confusing, well . . . you should have been there. There were times when you would be taking orders from three so-called plant managers and each order would be different from the others.

They used the number-three guy, the production manager, as the "hatchet man," the bad guy. When it was all over with and the smoke finally cleared, they retired the oldest plant manager for so-called health reasons—you know, number two, the one that had other plant managers report to him. They blamed all the problems and productions delays on the production manager—you know, number three, the hatchet man—and sent him to some other plant in Ohio, because General Motors needed him there more than we needed him at the new high-tech, up-and-coming Romulus plant. Well, guess what they were back to? The same clique, the same fucking clique, but now even stronger and more dangerous than ever before. They knew now they could handle anything and anybody, under any circumstance. They could lie and fuck with anybody and have their buddies swear to it as the truth and get away with it.

They would put people on jobs knowing they weren't good at that particular job or hated it. It got to the point where they would do it just for spite; you might say they were just practicing for future battle.

One time, another supervisor and I were standing in front of the general foreman offices when one of the superintendents walked up to us and said, "I see you're the only two guys that are still wearing ties."

You see, we were all given a choice. We could wear ties or not. They wanted everyone to look the same. Even the plant manager didn't wear a tie, except when he left to go downtown for a meeting. Then the tie came back on. You see this "game" that General Motors plays. They tell everyone to do these things like team concept: work together; look like each other; eat with each other; park in the same parking lot with each other. It's good for our image. We are all one . . . except when you go downtown. You'd better have that dark suit on, and you'd better have that tie on, and don't forget those "wing tips." (They now have what they call casual days, meaning a casual dress code, except on certain floors.)

Well, enough bullshit, do you want to know what happened in the tie incident? This eighth-level "boy wonder," from the hills, went on to say, "I know you had a choice on wearing ties, but I'd advise you two, if you want to be part of the team, to take those ties off." We both looked at each other, very pissed off, understanding now what team concept really meant, and then proceeded to take our ties off and throw them into the nearest garbage can. I never put another tie on until I left (escaped) that plant and I was told I could dress professionally again. This was intimidation and team concept at its best. Remember, whoever has the most power will be the biggest intimidator. Do you remember these names: John Delorian; H. Ross Perot? The same things happen at the top floors of the great General Motors Building as they do in the small job shops all around our country.

How could you have intimidation and team concept together in one place? Let me give you another example. The assembly line that was built to assemble the 4.3L engines that go into many of the trucks and vans built by General Motors was built in Turin, Italy. There was a group of hourly and salary people sent there in teams. The teams would spend eighteen days there and ten days home. We did this for eight months. Some times differed due to different situations. During the ten days that I was home,

I would spend it going over the things that were happening in Italy and also teaching team concept classes to the hourly and salary people. We taught in pairs. My partner was an hourly guy that was picked by the union. We were basically compatible, with the exception of the time he came into a classroom full of people and copped an attitude. While I was warming up the class he had a PMS attack and we actually had a shouting match in front of the class. I guess we really were compatible, because neither one of us knew how to back off. It was a mistake by both of us. I mean if we couldn't get along, how could we teach everybody to get along? Frustration was starting to take its course. For the last six months, both of us knew it wasn't working. Team concept was still . . . do what I say, and then you will be a team player. We never taught another class together after that incident. As a matter of fact, I never taught another class again at that facility. I look back at that situation and I ask myself, *Was I set up?*

Going to Italy was the highlight of the experiences of everyone associated with this project. It was the closest thing to team concept because everyone, both hourly and salary, was involved. While we were in Italy, the hourly guys were getting paid whatever their hourly partners that were in the same classification were getting paid at home. That means if an electrician was offered twelve hours a day, seven days a week at home, you would have to pay the electrician in Italy that amount, even if he didn't work that amount. What a deal. There's something wrong with the system, folks! We all basically worked a ten-hour day. Some more, some less. During my tour of eight months, we never went into the Comau facilities on a Saturday. The union there would not allow us in. We had electricians, toolmakers, pipe fitters, millwrights, machine repairmen, maintenance supervisors, and assembly supervisors. I was picked because one of my friends—let's call him Jack (a fictitious name)—told someone in higher management, "Hey, you should take Rino. He's Italian, he gets along with everyone, he's got twenty-some years of assembly experience, and he was picked as a coordinator.'' If it wasn't for Jack, I don't believe this would have happened. Jack was respected and liked by everyone, and I mean everyone. So I was chosen and I was Italy bound.

In the beginning of the project, we were told by higher management that when the various sections of the new assembly line became completed in Italy, the entire team would have to sign off on the sections or else it would not be accepted for release. We were told, by higher management, that before we could sign off on each section, the section would have to run one hour's worth of production with ''no'' rejects or else the section would not be accepted or released. Man, if this happened it was truly going to be a miracle. An assembly line actually being built with people who were actually going to work on it! It can happen; they did it in Lansing, Michigan, at the Oldsmobile Division, where the Quad Four engine line is located. That assembly line was built in the same place by the same people who worked on our line. The place was the Comau Metalworking Systems Division in Turin. There were a couple of differences between Oldsmobile's assembly line and ours. Their assembly line was built over a large area, and ours was to be built in a very compact area, similar to the way the Japanese build their assembly lines. We also were under a time constraint. It was now February, and the entire assembly line had to be built, run, disassembled, and shipped to America by August. It would have to be put together and be producing 4.3L engines by October 1. The Oldsmobile line did not have that kind of time constraint on them.

You would think that by building one assembly line already, you would know the problems that could and would occur dealing with a foreign country, their laws, and their customs. General Motors had had people in Italy for almost two years prior to this project. As a matter of fact, we were dealing with the same plant, the same people, the same everything, and it still turned into a proverbial "Chinese fire drill." Did we learn anything in the two years that Oldsmobile was over there? Did we listen with deaf ears when and if they tried to tell us vital information about dealing with a foreign country? Or maybe they were too interested in the beauty of Italy and more vacation time was spent there than business time. (They certainly all knew how to get their families there for vacation, while they were at work. Do you want to know who paid the majority of the families' tab? It's amazing what you can do on an expense report.)

The line was designed to build 100 to 120 engines an hour. That number was changed because it was very clear it was unattainable, as many things were going much slower than expected, and time was of the essence. The number was changed, not by the team, but by higher management.

The Italians were building the line just the way they were told and by the blueprint. The blueprints had many mistakes. These mistakes caused more changes, the changes caused even more delays, and the delays caused more problems. The new changes not only caused new money problems, but threatened the completion date would be much later than what was targeted. When the Italians said, "Here's the price of the changes to General Motors," the General would say, "No way." If you have ever built a home you know that there are various steps of payment that the contractor wants before the completion of the home. That's to ensure the contractor gets paid for everything he does, because there are usually many changes after you start building the product. It usually becomes more expensive. Well, after a couple of months of changes and no commitment from General Motors on the new price adjustments, the Italians stopped working on the project. Simple: no lire, no work! They knew the General was committed to a deadline, that they would have to do some quick negotiating. (The Italians obviously did their homework on how to deal with Americans and General Motors when they built the line for Oldsmobile.) Production of these engines were with the three major GM truck plants in the United States (Pontiac, Michigan; Shreveport, Louisiana; and Moraine, Ohio), and it would cost approximately a million dollars a day if this project didn't get off the ground in time. The stopping of the project would be a major financial problem, but it would also be one of General Motors' biggest manufacturing blunders of the decade. Perot had just told General Motors that the project dealing with Comau was not a good idea. That's all General Motors needed, another good jab in some editorial. Negotiations took place. More money by the Italians won. But now time was even more important. So higher management changed even more of the rules, not the team. An explanation of the changes was given to us, but the rule changes were not part of the team's decision. Now, if the sections would pass sixty an hour it was OK. Well, that also changed. Then it got down to thirty, and then less. Some sections never produced, not even, one good part. There were just too many changes to the prints, and no more time. The attitude of higher management was that we would make a list of all the problems from each section and the team would agree on the list of defects and then fix them when we got the sections back on the floor at the Romulus plant. BUUULLLSHIT! I knew it was too good to be true. Team concept, my ass. Needless to say, I wasn't buying it and I made a big deal about it. (Don't forget, I was teaching team concept back home at the plant and now, as far as I was concerned, my name and integrity were on the line.) I wouldn't sign anything unless it was done right. The team, with the exception of one other supervisor and a few hourly, was intimidated by higher management and their push to get things done their way. I told them, "You must stop making excuses, and now is the time you can show everyone you mean what you say. You're treating this the same way you treat assembly and manufacturing problems, like you always have. We, meaning everyone, must change your, higher management's, exact words."

If you have a problem building anything, whether it's an engine, a car, or whatever it may be STOP, STOP what you're doing and fix the problem. This has to be done. They do it in Japan, they do it at Saturn, and they do it in places where they have maximum efficiency and good-quality products. This system really works. It makes "QUALITY" work the very first time. At the present time, we realize we have a problem, we write down where the problem is so we can identify it, and we keep on building the defective products. We then put them in a "RE-PAIR" area, and work on them on overtime. Now everyone is in a hurry to get the job done, and not everyone knows how to fix the job, and you know that some of the parts that weren't fixed properly are going to get out to the customer! The same thing is happening here with this assembly line. Everything that we were doing and teaching was about "not" letting this happen anymore. Because some of us made such a big deal about it and because we wouldn't sign off on anything that wasn't done properly, we were dubbed by the project engineer and other higher management "non–team players" or "troublemakers." The project engineer made a phone call to the States and, the next thing we knew, we were back to Romulus, Michigan, for a "discussion" with our supervisors. When we got back to the plant, we were taken behind closed doors and were told how we weren't being "team players" and higher management proceeded to let us know how wrong we were in our actions and that we should stop acting like children. After the ass chewing, the other supervisor was not sent back to Italy for the rest of the final testing and disassembly. They told us they needed him there in Romulus! I was sent back after being instructed to keep my fuck-ing mouth shut and do what I was told. They wanted me to go back because I had more of a following of the hourly and salary people and more people were following my reactions. I went back, but it was the first time I didn't want to go back. I made a list of all the problems of every section that we attempted to run and gave this list to my supervisor and his supervisor and the project engineer. To this day, that line has never made the original product, with the original figures of manpower. Some of the original sections were removed, because there was too much downtime with some parts of the automation portions and they went back to good old "people power." Some sections, to this writing, still have the same problems, many years later. Production has been made, but with more people and a lot more overtime. Maybe I was wrong and I am looking at these things wrong, because the head project engineer not only made a great deal of money from this project (because of overtime), but was made out to be a superstar for pulling it off. He was what higher management wanted: a "yes-man" or, in their eyes, a real team player!

14

Ballistic Behavior

by Les Wheeler

The betrayal of the salaried employees (and, to a lesser degree, the hourly employees) has resulted in losses in loyalty, productivity, trust, and respect and promoted an overall decay in the work ethic of the bulk of the salaried employees still left at General Motors. At the top, higher management still thinks there's no problem. By "no problem" we mean that by their definition, they think they can still do anything they want with the salary workforce. They still are in the 1959 style of management and see no problem with it. They still think they don't need any cooperation from the troops. They can tell them to jump and they will. Of course they will. They still need their jobs. But now when they jump, it's not the usual three feet straight up and everyone keeps jumping over and over again until they are too tired to jump anymore. Now we all still jump, but it's a one-inch jump and it may not be up. It may be sideways (remember the GM shuffle, lots of motion, no progress), and it will only be one jump. Then, instead of getting on with it, everyone sits on their hands waiting for the next orders from on high.

You may ask just how General Motors has betrayed its workforce. Some of the items are: COLA (Cost of Living Adjustment), midpoint salary ratings, salary comparisons to competitors (if you can stretch this to include bank tellers and Kmart's personnel to an assembly line supervisor), personnel policies regarding beliefs and values, and pay for performance are just a few of the "plans" General Motors has put in place to use against its workforce.

First and foremost, among salaried employees, was the loss of the COLA (Cost of Living Adjustment) in the early 1980s. We were "deceived" by higher management that it was "good" for the "good" workers. Why be tied to an arbitrary adjustment that we had no control over when we could control our own destinies, work hard, and be rewarded with salary merit increases that would dwarf the COLA increases we had been receiving? As a point of fact, we had been receiving COLA and merit raises for quite a few years when this plan was rolled out. We might mention that this never affected executive bonuses. So, there never was any gain to be received by any of us. We lost out on COLA and then rarely ever saw the raises either. That was the plan from the git-go, folks; they never intended for us to receive the so-called PFP (Pay For Performance) raises on a yearly or timely basis. The only plan was to take back the COLA. To take it back without a revolt, they had to have some sort of a viable plan to replace it, ergo the PFP bullshit. The beauty of this is though hardly anyone (if anyone) believed it, what could you do? Nothing, nothing at all, because if you don't like it, you can quit! Real beliefs and values statement there, right! Just hope it doesn't happen to you so you can find out how helpless it feels to lose something and not be able to do anything about it.

Let's get off the track here for just a moment. We would not like any of you to think that comments like the above "you can quit" weren't made. They were, sometimes daily. Don't ever believe that bullshit from the top that they never knew what was going on. They knew; they always knew. Trying to get workers to quit had two facets to it. If they quit, great; if they don't, great. The second great is because now management knew that they had them. They could be intimidated from here on in. It's just like firing the air traffic controllers—you sure have the attention of the ones that are left, don't you? What do you think the odds are of them complaining too hard or too loudly again? Real slim, if they exist at all. But what are the odds of them working as hard as they used to before, coming in to work when they just don't feel that good? Consider the effect this management method had on the several thousand salaried employees at General Motors.

We know that some of you are thinking, *So what? I've never had a COLA. How can you complain that you've lost it?* Let's respond to those queries. At one time, the COLA was one of the great enticements or perks that General Motors was giving to people to be a salary employee and as an incentive to do a good job. Let me explain what this cost-of-living check was and why it was so important to the many salary employees that were not in the executive positions that came with high salaries and bonuses. The COLA was based on a percentage of your base salary and was given to each and every salary person in General Motors on a quarterly basis. It was like receiving a freebie check every three months for whatever you wanted to use it for. It was a separate means of planning your children's education, vacations, major purchases, the extras that normally you wouldn't have bought. The great part about getting COLAs was that about every eighteen months, on the average, you were also up for a merit increase. Now, let's take these things away from a standard of living that you were used to and depended on and here is what happens. You fall behind in your real purchasing power as we did year after year as we received very few or no raises and no COLA while our executives kept giving themselves record bonuses. The hourly employees still receive their COLA every week, because it is based on an hourly rate in accordance with their contract. The rumors in the office were that General Motors asked them to give it up to help out, but since the union could see that executive bonuses were still going out, they declined. General Motors is losing market share, closing plants, and laying off more and more hourly people while Mr. Smith and all of his executives are still giving themselves record bonuses and salary increases. Please pick an answer: A. No; B. Are you fucking nuts?; or C. All of the above.

The hourly people were also getting a perfect attendance bonus. This means that if you came to work every day except vacations and ''excused'' days off, by the end of the year you would be paid another $600. At the time of this contract, the UAW negotiators knew they had hooked a big one! It never did make a difference; the ones that came to work all the time still come to work all the time and the ones that were always absent still are. Let us also tell you that there is no bonus for salaried employees for perfect attendance. This is not intended to be a knock on or at hourly employees anywhere. They agreed to the contract just as GM management did. To complain about the contract after you agreed to it as GM management has done repeatedly in the past, does at present, and will continue to do in the future is in very poor taste, to say the least.

So, it's one thing to take the COLA away if it's being replaced, but to take it away and replace it with virtually nothing creates a pay cut. If your raises aren't over 5–6 percent per year, you lose ground to inflation and eventually you can never catch up to the standard of living you had before. When you lose ground like this, it's tough to buy the cars and trucks you are helping to produce.

Around this same time frame, General Motors began to tell us that we were all overpaid. New guidelines were implemented setting the midpoint of salaries, based on classification and job description. Strange, but they kept telling us that the jobs and salaries we were being compared to were all automotive. Based on their comparison, which were all unbiased of course, we were usually categorized as being way past the midpoint of the accepted salary range for the type of job we were doing and therefore couldn't get a raise. This was not a new trick by General Motors; they tried the same crap in the late sixties and early seventies, with varying results then, too. Unfortunately, we have the list of jobs they compared us to, and we're sorry to say that we just don't see the comparison between a front-line supervisor and a bank teller or a clerk at a retail store. The pressures and responsibilities are in no way comparable between these jobs.

Midpoint salary rating also took on a very interesting twist in that General Motors spent big bucks to train all their supervisors in the concept that every department was a normally distributed work group. This meant that if you had five people in your department, one was great, three were average, one was below average, and the supervisor should be taking steps to fire the below-average individual.

In a nutshell (versus a nuthouse, which is what General Motors is), that means if you had five of the best workers anywhere in the world working for you yesterday, you don't today. One of them is still outstanding, but three of them are now only average and one of them became stupid overnight! Now, just when you thought it couldn't get worse, it does. It's better to be one of the average workers because (by the way, forget PFP, because it doesn't exist anymore and you'd better not ask about it either) the outstanding person can't get a raise, as he is over the midpoint salary range. The catch 22 here is that the average workers can get a raise until they, too, are over the magical midpoint when their performance has earned them too much to be eligible for a raise. But, of course, they will have to continue to work at that higher level of output for no monetary incentives, including no COLA, or risk being the bottom person of the five and have someone trying to fire them every day for the rest of their career. What a belief and values kind of place to work!

15

So Where Does All the Money Come From?

by Les Wheeler

It's about money. Everything is about money.

Where *does* all the money come from? One of the more intriguing problems facing General Motors, and it has always been this way, is how we spend our money internally. From time immemorial, it has been the rule that you had to spend your budget or lose it. If you estimated that you would spend $7,000 in your tooling account for the year and then didn't, you would be allotted a smaller budget the following year. So any fool would never let that happen. If you saw that you were underspent for the year in November, you just bought a heck of a lot of something that was on hand in the crib every day during the month of December. I don't care what it was, twelve dozen gloves or whatever. It didn't make any difference. You had to buy something to use up your budget, or you wouldn't have it next year.

Where is the incentive to improve here? There isn't any. If you improve, you lose. You would then lose head count and that equated to power and that was bad. Loss of power (or turf, as Rino likes to call it) is a no-no at General Motors. You do everything in your power to see that it doesn't happen even if it's bad for the organization, and that's what we're talking about here. If you lose sight of the organization and worry only about your power base, the organization suffers in the long run. That's another problem: We don't pay anyone to be successful in the long run. We only reward short-term gains, because most managers won't even be in that particular job in a year anyway, so why worry about the future? The future is now and we have to pay dividends now. That's what our investors expect and demand. They expect and demand that because that's what we told them they would receive from us. It is of little consequence, to any of them, if we go out of business, because they will just write off the losses and reinvest their money in some other company and probably make money from the loss. Of course, this does not in any way take into account the loss of jobs or the effect it has on anyone's life. It would be true to say that they don't care. Management may not care too much if General Motors goes under, because they all have their own "golden parachutes" and it's not going to be a problem for them, as someone, for some strange reason, will always give them a job. We say strange reason because we can't understand why anyone would want to hire someone who just drove his company out of business. It doesn't make any sense at all unless you realize that, sadly, they, too, think it isn't them, it's everyone else who didn't do their job, never the top management. Sad, but true.

It's a sad turn of events, as the budgeting policy once worked, when we were a car company selling cars and we made big profits, in spite of ourselves. In those days, we never had to worry about satisfying the customer. We're not even sure if anyone even worried about the customer. We did things that we wanted to, when we wanted to, and how we wanted to. "Full speed ahead, damn the torpedoes . . . ," or forget the customer, do what we want, they will have to buy it and if they don't like it, there is a guy, right now, being treated in an unsatisfactory manner by Ford and he will come here and we will promise him anything and deliver nothing that we promised (obviously, the setting for the politician's code of ethics). That's part of the problem surrounding the money also. The money never comes out of our pocket, like it does at home. It comes from General Motors' pockets, and they have deep pockets, so don't worry. Now we know our pockets are, in fact, not that deep, in part because we spent it all on some insane acquisitions and then spent even more to silence someone who made more sense than the rest of the board combined. Which, obviously, made sense to someone who has since retired with a golden parachute of his own, worth a cool million per year. But when you make the rules to fit your needs and not those of the organization, things like this happen.

There is no incentive to improve because the money comes from some bottomless pit somewhere and if you don't spend the money, they take it away. We have budgets for scrap and repair, and God forbid if you don't scrap enough or repair enough materials along the way. Coupled with the thought that it's not your money, even though you work here, too, makes it dangerous thinking to try to improve. It should be the job of every person within General Motors to improve his job or department every day of every year. That doesn't mean cutting personnel or services either. It means that you should be thinking of ways to improve your area, by doing more work or offering more services with the same amount of people and not having to add people to do more work. Doing more work with the same amount of personnel is an increase in productivity. Unfortunately, it is not perceived as being the good or right thing to do. After all, "The guys downtown said to cut personnel; they didn't say to increase productivity. If increasing productivity had been the goal, we would have rolled over the opposition long ago." Of course, if we had, then our government would have stepped in and stopped us in our tracks, because of antitrust laws or what have you. We sometimes think if we are our own worst enemy, then the government is definitely in second place and not too far behind us either. This is sad, but true. The game was to make short-term profits and spend all the money you said you would or people would be all over you in a New York minute. How can you run a business like that, you ask? Easy, the pockets are deep and it's not my money, it's theirs and they've got a lot of it, so don't worry.

We alluded earlier in the chapter to people spending money so they wouldn't lose their budget for next year, and it's the truth. If you want to think of how stupid that is, the next time you have an extra ten bucks, go to the store and buy ten gallons of milk or ten pounds of any kind of nails, as you may need them someday for something. Don't worry about saving anything or some other stupid thought like that. Just go ahead and spend; there will always be more tomorrow. Remember, the well never runs dry and there's no reason or reward to save. Now, as the well is running dry and there ain't no more where that came from, we continue to see the double standard within the organization.

We, along with every other low-level person in the organization, are being told that we have to pay for our own health care benefits. That may not seem like a big deal to you, especially if you have been paying for yours all along. But, to us, it's a pay cut. It's a take-away from what we have had. It's a shot in the back from the same people who have told us time and time again that we are their most important resource. It's just one more lie to add to all the others. It's even worse when you remember that we were promised that we wouldn't notice the loss of our cost-of-living pay, because they were going to give us merit raises to compensate for that take-away. That sounds like a good deal, but somewhere along the way that money never materialized for most of us trying to do the job and being too busy to kiss someone's ass to get it. If you weren't part of the good old boys' network, it just didn't happen, and if it did, the raises weren't very regular or very good. That's at our level; executives have no problem overcompensating themselves with increases in salary and bonuses. It's really strange that I'm being asked to save a nickel here and a penny there while my bosses are standing on the roof shoveling off thousand-dollar bills as fast as they can.

It simply serves to reinforce the old "us versus them" mentality. It's OK for us to save pennies while they spend dollars on themselves. In one organization, an edict came down that everyone would have to buy their own business cards. Now, that's going to save a lot of bucks, probably enough to build a new plant in Mexico or Korea. At the same time, it's not a problem to pay three hourly employees to wash and gas the vehicles of the top executives. I guess, in my wildest dreams, I can see that it is a necessary perk to keep top managers on the job, and it might not be that bad if you were paying these guys the same wages as the guy in the car wash. But we're not. We're paying them top dollar to do this, at least the same rate as an assembler, if not higher, because we have probably made this a special classification so they could never be bumped from this job. What I really mean is that I can never see paying anyone to wash and gas my car, because I'm too busy to do it myself. Especially when times are tough and we need every dime we can get our hands on.

For that matter, these guys keep those vehicles parked in heated or air-conditioned garages during working hours. That's an interesting story in itself. You see, top executives never ever drive a car like the one you or I might drive. The people in charge pretty much guarantee that they will never be inconvenienced by some problem, such as a window not going down or back up, a rattle in the dash, or some other dumb problem. They're too busy to have to deal with a problem like that. So what does General Motors do? They pay other people to inspect and repair these vehicles before the executives ever see them. Depending upon who you are, in the organization, it may take anywhere from one to three days to verify that the vehicle is OK for use. Now, why don't we do that to every vehicle and not just for the shooters? I don't know; perhaps General Motors can tell us. It seems like they are a touch too insulated from the real world already and we take it one step further by the minute.

16

What Budget? Honey, the Limo's Here!

by Rino Pagnucco

The comptroller's wife was yelling, "Honey, the limo's here!"

The comptroller yelled back, "Wait a minute, honey! I have to finish reading this article in the *Wall Street Journal* that says we, at General Motors, have to get rid of 1,200 more salary heads and 100,000 more hourly people in order to survive in the automotive industry." The comptroller exclaimed, "Wow, look at this! Stempell's a goner; John Smith and Hogland may be in."

Now what's wrong with this story? In October 1992, the great American corporate shakeup was happening.

I don't know if those were the exact words that were said at the Pontiac Motor division comptroller's house on the day that he "had" to leave for a Pontiac Dealership Participation Masters Outing in Florida. When I had heard about one of our divisional heads taking a limousine to the airport only one day after my boss was telling his staff about cost cutting and how General Motors can't afford to give everyone raises this year, I was again confused by the signals that our "leaders" were sending us. This is just one of many everyday excessive spending habits that continue to go on, regardless of what's happening in the total picture. The thinking here is that: *It's not my division or department that's causing the red ink, so I will continue to spend.*

The same thing is happening in our country. We have senators and house representatives that continue to say, "It's not my state or region that is causing the deficit, so why should I stop spending?" In this particular incident, here's the problem, as I see it. Divisional comptrollers not only make pretty damn good money, but they get a lot of benefits that go way beyond the norm. General Motors is in the midst of falling on its ass, the chairman of the board is ousted due to the flow of red ink, the signs of doom and gloom are in the air, and we still can't get some people's attention. I don't mean just middle management; I mean from the heads of departments and the zone and branch managers to divisional leaders.

In this particular instance, a limousine came to pick up the divisional comptroller to drive him to Detroit Metro Airport. He couldn't have driven his own car? Which, by the way, he gets for free. Maybe he thought General Motors would have to pay for the airport parking and twenty-six dollars for one week might be a bit too much. Or he probably thought that he would have to take the shuttle bus with the "common folk." There could be a real possibility that he would have to fetch "his own luggage." No wonder he took the limo!

Let's go back a minute; let's talk perks here. This guy not only gets a free new car; he gets a new one every 3,000 miles. You better believe it's never a subcompact either. He doesn't have to insure it or fuel it or wash it or maintain it; he just has to drive it. It's fueled and washed every day. I guess he doesn't even have to drive it; after all, he got a limo to take him to the airport.

More perks. Let me explain what the Masters Outing is. It's a reward. A reward that every division gives to the top 100 dealers reaching their sales objectives. The Masters Outing includes wining and dining for certain divisional employees and their spouses, along with the winning dealers, salespeople, and their spouses. All expenses paid. When I say all expenses paid, I mean "ALL"

133

expenses paid. All meals, drinks, rooms, travel, cars, and entertainment. Entertainment means anything from big-name comedians for a night of jokes, to big-name speakers or Las Vegas type shows for everyone. At one event, they canceled one of the entertainers and hired Lee Greenwood, because country singing and his songs of patriotism were more popular at the time! Due to contractual obligations, they still had to pay the other performer who was canceled!

Oh, by the way, if your wife needs her hair done, don't worry, the General will pick up the tab. Entertainment during the day is anything from as much free golf as you can stand to parasailing. Or "get on one of those four sailboats that we hired for anyone that wants to go sailing." There were times when some of those sailboats never left the dock, but they had to be there just in case someone wanted to use them. Eating is anything you can imagine; just order it. I can guarantee it won't be a grand slam breakfast from Denny's. I can also guarantee it's not at the twenty-six-to-thirty-four-dollar-a-day meal "cap" rate (dependent on the city) that General Motors limits its traveling employees to.

I'm not talking about a couple of people here; I'm talking about a hundred–plus people. I'm not talking about one day here; I'm talking about a week. It would have taken around two hundred thousand dollars to cancel everything. Again, I know we had this planned in advance, and it was a contest. I know we still need to do promotions, and I truly believe we still have to spend some money. But just to say, "We have had this planned for a long time; let's get on with it," is just plain ridiculous and selfish. You see, this sends out a message to the lower levels of the corporation that there are problems in "DESIGNATED AREAS ONLY." I'm not sure all the amounts are correct in this particular situation, but they're damn close. Some are higher; some are lower. I still can't believe the guy "in charge" of the division's financial picture rented a fucking limo! Boy, that's above and beyond the commonsense level of spending.

This happens at all divisions, not just this one. Buick Motor Division virtually spends hundreds of thousands of dollars on its Buick Open Golf Classic. The budget thinking of "spend it or lose it" is still there. It has always been the theory that "it's GM money, not mine. They've got a lot of it, so why save it or economize at all?" This kind of thinking has been there forever. I can remember back in the early seventies when I was a young general foreman and I was first introduced to a departmental "green sheet." I was told by a plant engineer that this was my budget and I should spend it. I didn't get a raise for staying below my budget or saving money; I ACTUALLY GOT SOME FLACK! The amount that you spent was a guide on how much you would get for the next year's budget. It's been twenty-five years and we're still thinking that way.

I was at a meeting in Kansas City a couple of months before the shakeup happened, and the managers were stressing how much trouble General Motors was in. The very next sentence they were apologizing because they had to cut down on the accommodations. You see, the Kansas City meeting wasn't on a beach or on a golf course, where they were used to having their "seminars." They were having trouble with the people in internal controls asking why a seminar had to be in cities that ended in *Beach*, like Myrtle Beach. Yes, they are doing better, but they are still not focusing in on what needs to be done. In Kansas City, in my opinion one of God's best-kept secrets, the meeting started on Sunday so everyone could meet each other over "hors d'oeuvres" promptly at six o'clock. Here's a six-day meeting for over a hundred people, including secretaries and all the "CONTRACT PEOPLE." Flights for everyone, three meals a day for everyone, plus snacks at break time twice a day. Snacks . . . chocolate-covered strawberries, Dove ice cream bars, pastries, fresh-cut fruits, and hot and cold beverages. There was no alcohol served at this function, and they were very apologetic over this, but after all they had to cut back. Though, after hours, there was this place, called the family room, and that's where you could meet and play cards and have a drink. Did I say drink? Magically, there were three or four fifths of booze on the counter; help yourself.

Even though we were now called a corporate section, we were still run by the very powerful people from another division. Let's just call them the "HEARTBEAT" people. Some of the people that came from this division were a little upset because they weren't going to get a day of golf in and there wasn't any booze and they weren't near a beach. I didn't want to mention this again, but since I'm on a roll here, we also included the "RETREADS" in our meetings—you know, those retirees or contract people that aren't really there but really are.

We have many facilities in the Detroit area owned by General Motors that we could have used to cut our expenses considerably. We still would have to fly people in, but the majority of the people lived in the Detroit area. Don't worry, as I am writing this segment I also have to get ready for our next seminar . . . in St. Louis. SAME SHIT, DIFFERENT DAY!

It's difficult for me, here at the bottom, to listen to our supervisors and divisional heads preach about how much trouble we are in financially, how it's up to us to save the nickels and dimes when our leaders are on the roof shoveling hundreds of thousands of dollars off the top. Picture it this way. Here's the owner of a "widget" company, who pulls up to his shop in a brand-new Cadillac STS and gets out, gold hanging all over his freshly tanned body, just returning from a two-week cruise in Hawaii. He has an important announcement to make, so he gets everyone together, from the sweeper to the plant manager. He then starts telling everyone, "We all have to sacrifice a little more. There aren't going to be any more raises for a while. All of you will have to start paying for a portion of your medical benefits, and we are all going to have to try harder in these lean and hard times TO BE MORE EFFICIENT.'' God, when are we going to wake up?

Wait; there's more. How about training programs and consultants? Let's just piss away some more money! OK, General Motors hires people to train us and consult with us from outside firms that come with some pretty hefty fees. The odd thing here is that General Motors hires these people to find out how to ''save money'' and be more lean and mean in today's competitive market. We, at General Motors, have a training program and staff that is one of the best in the world. So why don't we listen to them? Why don't we walk like we talk? I mean if you are not going to listen to these high-priced consultants for the big dollar, why don't you just not listen to your own people for a little bit of money? By the way . . . they both say the same thing. Wait; wait . . . I've got an idea. We should give every executive or manager in charge a hearing test, because they ain't fucking listening!

Whether you are a single person living in an apartment or a single parent or the parents of five children, you still live within a budget. You don't tell the kids you don't have enough money to send them to camp and then send yourself and Mom to Las Vegas for a week.

There was a divisional head that once sent all of his associates ''musical'' Christmas cards. Yes, ladies and gentlemen, just open that baby up and HO, HO, HO, Merry Christmas. A nice little jingle came out of the card to the tune (no pun intended) of only $40,000. DO YOU THINK HE HAD TO PAY FOR THEM? HEY, WHEN YOU BOUGHT THAT NEW CAR . . . YOU BOUGHT THEM! The examples go on and on. This attitude that has been around so long is something very hard to break. Contrary to the beliefs of so many people, the new board of directors may be the right people to run the business. Yes, they aren't car people, but they are businesspeople. There are still some people not quite middle management but within supervisory positions who are upset because they can't play golf on a working weekday or they question why we don't have booze at seminars anymore. Some of these people haven't bought a car in twenty years, but they bitch about "those fucking hourly people" who are going on strike because of unsafe working conditions or the reality of losing their jobs across the border for "cheap" labor when they have never been in a factory in their lives. They haven't seen or understand the other side of the coin. These are the same people, in many cases, that have never had to take a new car back to a dealership and put up with some of the "crap" that Mr. and Mrs. Average New Car Buyer have to put up with after they buy a new car, taking into consideration that the dealership promised all those wonderful things that they would do and cover "IF" something should go wrong with the vehicle.

Some of the perks we get are truly gratifying, but we take them for granted and when some people abuse them, they get upset when they lose them. If you allow room in your plans for ABUSING THE SYSTEM, YOU DESERVE WHAT YOU GET! Perks! You take an airline that gives you frequent flyer mileage, your hotel gives you points, your rental car gives you additional miles and upgrades, and so on and so on. IT'S ABOUT GREED. HOW MUCH IS ENOUGH?

It may be cheaper to stay somewhere else just as nice and it may be cheaper to fly another airline, but you don't get those frequent flyer miles with them. You see, the guidelines say that it's OK to use the more expensive airlines and it's OK to use the more expensive hotel because they are in the "preferred" status chosen by General Motors. I am not saying that we have to stop spending . . . we just have to start spending "smarter."

17

Privacy versus Trust

by Rino Pagnucco

What is the violation of privacy or the invasion of privacy? Unfortunately, the question that has come up during working hours is: While working, does every second of your time belong to your employer? When you are "on the clock," so to speak, does this give your employer the right to say, "While you are on the clock working for me, your ass is mine!" I mean if you get hurt or you die on the job, your employer has to take care of you. It's kind of like living at home when you were sixteen years old and coming in at one o'clock in the morning on a school night—your father felt he had the right to kill you! How many times did you hear, "It's my house, these are my rules, and as long as you are going to live here you have to obey these rules, because I brought you into this world and I have the right to take you out!" If you are a teenage girl and you keep a diary and you live under "that" roof, does that give your parents the right to read your diary?

Where does the invasion of privacy begin or end? Do you belong to your employer 100 percent, from the time you clock in to the time you clock out? Or if you are on salary and you travel for the company and are on the road twenty-four hours a day, are you a slave to the company after normal working hours?

The company's theory is that your conduct is their business, because you are there representing the company even after working hours.

It has gotten to the point where many companies have told their managers to start spying on certain employees, especially the so-called known troublemakers or non–team players, spying to the point of following certain employees into the bathroom, hiding behind corners until the employee went into a stall and then waiting a few minutes and going into the next stall, to stand on the toilet and look over the top to see if he was really going to the bathroom or just taking a break. I'm sorry to say that this really happens, folks. Do you remember what happened before the post office killings in 1992 and 1993? It was this kind of intimidation by their employers that led certain people to snap.

While I was working for General Motors there was a rumor circulating around that some of our telephone calls through the VME (voice mail system) were being tapped and listened to by certain managers. I mean why not? You were leaving a message on a tape recorder, and even if you marked the message private, they could still get into your messages. If you don't believe me about tapes, it's sad that it's too late to ask Richard Nixon. If it goes on tape, there will be a way to access it. There is also a system on your computers, normally called "E" mail, which allows you to talk to each other and send messages back and forth through the computer. The rumor was that higher management was going into this system and intercepting some of the messages. Let me tell you that I couldn't prove any of these accusations, but because of certain incidents that happened to certain people and by talking to certain EDS (Electronic Data Systems) personnel I believe that even though it is unethical, it certainly is possible.

On July 10, 1993, at our apartment just outside Detroit, I was watching the Channel Two eleven o'clock news when a commercial came on and a "news tip" was announced. The news tip given by one of the news anchormen warned people that they should be wary of what they put on their work computers, that more and more companies are admitting to going into and seeing what is written in these computers after hours, when employees go home for the evening. It just gave me more proof that this type of behavior by higher management is allowed and is happening in many of our companies today.

So you want more proof that this type of activity is practiced by our employers? On July 21, 1993, on NBC, *First Person with Maria Shriver* came on saying, "Remember Big Brother?" This was a hard-hitting documentary on how our bosses spy on us. All is fair in love and war, as long as you are the boss. It is OK to use any type of tactic, which can include urine tests, cameras in the locker room, personality or psychological testing, listening to voice mail, or looking at electronic mail in computers, according to some. Spying has become a new way of doing business. The testers will state that everything is confidential, but many have found out that this is not true. The testing is there to manipulate and, in some cases, terminate employees. As an employee, you should never, ever assume you have any rights ... because you're not the boss. If, by chance, you are not the top boss, you'd better watch your ass, because Big Brother is watching you!

So, why is it that the tools the companies give you to do your job, such as the voice mail system, are presented to you as perks (letting your family have the number to aid them in communicating with you when you're on the road), but in reality are turned into weapons with which you can commit suicide? Is it another part of the package to entice someone to take the job, and when they are done using you, if that time ever comes, or the time comes when there is a "reduction in workforce," these are the things that management can and will hold against you to get rid of you? I mean you can look at it this way: my handy-dandy Swiss Army knife was made for survival, but you can

141

certainly kill with it, if need be. I guess you could go on and on with just about anything if you look at it with a negative attitude, but when you are consistently put in those situations and with the many changes that are happening in the business today, it's hard not to always be on the defensive. We talked about trust and respect earlier in the book. When you have lost this among your employees, you have also lost a commitment from the people. You are then running the business on fear and intimidation.

We had another one of our meetings again in the second week of July. Of course, it was in Dallas and, of course, they wanted everyone to be there on Sunday for dinner. Our Canadian counterparts couldn't be there, because their management said it was too expensive and besides, we were all going to have another quarterly meeting for one week in Troy, Michigan, in two weeks. Yes, you heard me right, in just two weeks we were going to have "another" week of breakfasts, lunches, and dinners and have meetings and breaks for everyone and the agendas for both meetings were almost the same. We still have people in General Motors in control that think General Motors just has too much money!

Our director had this bitch session one night in Dallas because he wanted everyone to be able to say whatever they wanted without any reprisal from anyone. One of the reasons for this meeting in Dallas was because a lot of mistrust and unhappiness was starting to show in our organization. So, to set the tone of this meeting, the director started out by telling everyone at the meeting that he did not want to hear any more statements about how everything was "Chevrolet" and that if someone were to mention that again, this boss would personally go to that person and ask for his transfer, and he would make sure it happened. For the past year, everything was based on the Chevrolet way of doing business. All of the newest announced promotions were of the Chevy people. There was only one supervisor left that wasn't a Chevrolet person, and he was living on the edge.

Well, you can imagine how the rest of the meeting went. The director was in complete control and only heard the things he wanted to hear. General Motors has always said that their people were their most important asset. So, why do the bosses have to listen to our telephone conversations or go into our computers and see what we are saying to one another? Why does anyone have to be followed? Why do we allow someone to make up a story about someone and then have someone swear that it really happened for the sake of firing the other guy? You have heard me say this before: "The first liar wins." When it comes to having scruples and morals, some of our managers, not only in General Motors but everywhere, have absolutely none, zip, zero. What is really frightening is that top management wants to hire them. They actually go looking for these kinds of people. They are no better than professional hit men.

There are many laws on privacy, but sometimes managers become so selfish that they don't care about the law. They develop such tunnel vision that they can destroy someone's character and career. At this point, they don't even care about what is best for the company. So what if the case ends up in court and the employee wins? It's still going to take two to five years to complete the legal process. Right now, the companies feel justified in what they are doing.

Is your private life really yours?

18

Tora! Tora! Tora!; or, Pearl Harbor II

by Rino Pagnucco

Well, there I was again sitting in another airport waiting for another airplane. To while the time away, I started reading a book called *Rising Sun*, by Michael Crichton. My partner had given me this book and told me, "Read this; it will enlighten you." Well, it enlightened me alright; it opened my eyes even more to the reality of what is happening in our society. It was a real eye opener. If there was anyone that advocated, "Be American . . . buy American," I would have to say I was on the top of the list, along with Sam Walton (founder of Wal-Mart), my partner, my brother Nelson, and my cousin Roy. I think it would be safe to say that you probably have only heard of Sam Walton and not any of these other guys. But these other guys are just like many of the hundreds of thousands of Americans who are just trying to succeed in their everyday living by working hard, following the laws of the land, and paying their taxes. They are doing everything that they were told they should do to be good Americans and succeed in America. Now, all of a sudden, they are wondering why they are working harder and longer hours but aren't getting any further ahead. Why has it become so very difficult and frustrating beyond belief to realize that we can't even keep our heads above water, let alone get ahead?

I believe that every American who is truly for seeing General Motors, Ford, Chrysler, and any other American-owned business and America itself succeed needs to read my book and also Michael Crichton's book *Rising Sun* (1992). The book and the movie of the same name were, in my opinion, very different from each other. The movie was good, but the book was better. We need to wake up the sleeping giant known as America and make it the proud and prosperous country it once was. We need to wake up General Motors and make it the auto giant it once was. If we don't all change and wake up now, before long whenever you see the title "United States of America" it will have the trademark on the lower right-hand side that says: "MADE IN JAPAN"!

If you think you have heard these words before, you probably have. In 1970, Twentieth Century, now Twentieth Century Fox, Film Corporation made a movie about the bombing of Pearl Harbor. It was called *Tora! Tora! Tora!* The movie re-created the attack on Pearl Harbor and the events leading up to the attack. "Tora! Tora! Tora!" I believe, is the Japanese signal to attack. It was what the Japanese kamikaze pilots were saying just before they committed suicide by letting the planes they flew crash into the American warships, using themselves and their aircraft as bombs. They only filled the planes up with enough fuel to go one way. They were so committed to winning the war for their nation, they knew they were going to give up their lives. Now that's commitment!

The Chevrolet Geo Storm has already adopted the logo "MADE IN JAPAN," along with many other so-called American automobiles. The so-called yuppies of America that I would like to talk about are truly the "kamikaze" pilots that are silently yelling, *Tora! Tora! Tora!* as they continue to buy their Hondas, Toyotas, Lexuses, and BMWs. Presently, it usually takes two, husband and wife, to go to work to own a home. Not just any home, it has to be the one in Rochester Hills or Birmingham, Michigan, or some other up-and-coming high-tax community that would be the "in" place to live. Every major city has these "yuppie" suburban neighborhoods. Who takes care of the children when it takes both parents to go to work? Well, in many cases it's the grandparents. Come on, boys and girls, give them a break; they already brought up a family! Or is it a child care center? If we keep buying the way we are buying, we eventually won't have any choice. Let me give you an example of what I call a kamikaze pilot or yuppie, one and the same as far as I'm concerned.

There was this guy who used to live next door to me in Canton, Michigan. Nice guy, nice wife—she also worked—just an all-around nice couple. So, anyway, this guy worked for EDS. Last time I heard, EDS was part of General Motors. Well, he went out and bought a brand-new car. Nothing wrong with that, except it was a Honda. You know, for the longest time, I kept seeing this car, but I couldn't figure out what kind of a car it was. Well, one day, he stopped his car to say hello while I was cutting the grass. To my amazement, I saw the Honda trademark. I even went so far as to ask him if he had quit General Motors. He told me he works for EDS, not General Motors. Damn, I always thought we were a team of one, silly me. I guess I should have read the book *Irreconcilable Differences*, by Doron Levin, sooner than I did. Perot versus General Motors. When I finally did read the book, I had a better idea why EDS personnel act the way they do. The sad part is that EDS doesn't even think they are part of General Motors. There is a reason for this. Even today, EDS management is still being "bullied"—or should I say fucked with?—by the old, very intimidating, 1959 style of GM management that still runs the business and has never accepted EDS in their world. The problem is still within! The injustice here is that both sides have turned my old neighbor into a true kamikaze pilot. He is on a mission, a mission to destroy, no matter what the cost. He doesn't even know he is doing it. He truly believes he is doing the right thing. This guy is not alone;

there are millions of Americans who are doing the same thing, and they truly believe they aren't doing anything wrong. These people have lost control over mine, yours, our children's, and their children's future. You know, I heard one lady go as far as to say, "Well, it won't make a difference in my lifetime, so what!" This kind of selfishness makes me want to throw up . . . preferably on her!

Loyalty to the companies that we work for and to the country we live in is slipping away at a very fast pace. Americans are becoming more and more dependent not only on Japan, but on Mexico and many other foreign countries. If this guy from EDS continues to buy his Japanese cars and if one of my former supervisor associates, who still works for General Motors, still drives his Jaguar or the hourly machine operator who won a top suggestion award at his GM plant ran out and bought a Porsche, then Michigan's Dr. Kevorkian ain't got nothing on these kamikaze pilots regarding suicide.

Now, with NAFTA being passed by the Clinton administration, I truly believe the new commander in chief of the kamikaze pilots of the world has to be Bill Clinton. His thinking on NAFTA is now spreading into the American society and the world. In my opinion, President Clinton doesn't understand the ramifications of this treaty. I am telling you the problems that we have today and have had in the past, both in the automotive industry and in our country, we have done to ourselves. It's not what others have done to us. We are destroying ourselves!

Let me give you another example. I was in a GM dealership in Charleston, South Carolina, and I happened to notice that one of the part companies that delivered parts on a daily basis to the dealership was delivering them in a foreign pickup truck. Here's where the line "you can't see the forest for the trees" came from. This is the problem as I see it. We have two wrongs here. One, we have a business that depends on an American business that sells American-made products but doesn't support "their" product. Now don't get me wrong, I am not trying to be one-sided here. I wouldn't be so upset if he drove in with a Ford or a Dodge. I am sure he delivers to those car dealerships also. But is the hidden signal that this driver is sending that he has to use a "dependable" foreign truck to deliver parts to an American dealership that is selling "undependable" cars and trucks? We just continue to do it to ourselves. Two, the American companies don't support their own automobiles. As I looked over this dealership, everything began to look wrong. A Pontiac-GMC dealership that also sells Porsches, with a Toyota driving up to deliver parts. This goes on so often, we just take it for granted. That dealer should have gone to that guy, made him a deal to sell him a comparable GMC truck at a lower price, and if repairs to the truck were ever necessary, the dealership would handle them at discount prices. Or they should at least inform the parts dealer that he should buy any American-made vehicle or not do business with this dealership anymore. I know this sounds selfish and is a difficult task, but we have to start somewhere. I know it can be done because I have seen it done.

A gentleman named Roger Penske is probably best known for owning topnotch racing cars. He took an ailing and failing GM division called Detroit Diesel from the cellar that General Motors drove it into, turned it back around, and made it come back beyond the major-market-share business that it once was. The people that work there respect him and believe in the product they work on and build and, most important, respect their customers. How did he bring it back? By being a smart businessman and using the "team concept" approach. Whether you race cars, build cars, build championship sports teams, or make and build widgets, it has to be a "TEAM EFFORT." He got everyone involved. He not only spoke, but he listened. He knew that if he wanted to become successful in this business, everyone had to share not only in accomplishing the goals that had been set and agreed upon by everyone, but also in the profits. You see, when General Motors owned Detroit Diesel some of the companies that delivered material to them were using trucks with non–Detroit Diesel engines. Well, Roger recognized this and told these companies that he would make them a deal. If they wished to continue to receive millions of dollars from "the new" Detroit Diesel, then he wanted to make sure that the companies receiving money from him would also agree to use his engines in the trucks that were bringing products into his plants. At a deal, of course. He would also give them good warranties and good service agreements and would go as far as to properly train the trucking companies' mechanics. This also performed one other major factor. It told the people who worked there and saw these trucks come and go that they really built a damn good product. It motivated them to continue to do a good job. Now the ones that didn't agree and continued to use the competition's engines to deliver material to his doorsteps no longer did business with him. Simple, it works both ways, and you have to remember to be fair both ways. I'll put in your pocket, and you put some back into my pocket. He did such a good job of making and keeping commitments, he told the workforce (that was the old disgruntled and betrayed GM workforce) that if they would start taking pride in where they work and start putting quality back into their work he would also share the profits equally with everyone. The people took care of the quality, and Roger took care of the delivery. Talk about walking like you talk! By the end of the first year, everyone got a profit sharing check. You talk about making a believer out of someone.

Every one of us can do this. Just be fair and use good judgment. Quoting the people at Toyota, "Business is war." The dealership in Charleston is really doing an injustice to themselves and the community by supporting the foreign companies that have increased our unemployment lines. The owner of the parts store (the commodore) is sending his driver (the kamikaze pilot) out in our community and silently saying, *Tora! Tora! Tora!*

Maybe we should all be like my big brother; maybe I should say older brother. He operates a small fabrications shop that is trying to get ahead. He said that it used to be fun to go to work, it was a challenge to try to get ahead, but now the business has never been worse. He says General Motors has been one of the most difficult customers to deal with, but they are also one of his last few customers and they've got him between a rock and a hard spot. He has to abide by all of "their" rules, which means having the latest technology and computers; otherwise he won't be qualified to make GM parts, which really means that General Motors wants the best quality that money "can't" buy! You must also realize that the equipment that General Motors wants in his shop is very expensive; plus he has to be a competitive bidder, which really means he has to be one of the low bidders. Here's what I mean by a "rock and a hard spot." Bid low (which equals a very small profit margin), so you can keep the customer that pays the bills, but now it's so low that you can't afford to buy the high-tech equipment. So, in order to buy the high-tech equipment you must skim somewhere else, so you "lay off" some more workers and then work longer hours for less pay. Then, when it comes time to pay the bills on time, General Motors takes their sweet old ass time. Why do they get to make all the rules and take their time paying the bills? Because they are in command and they know it. No sense bitching, because you need that customer. Truly a "no win" situation.

What gives us a false impression is that many of the GM employees that are left work a tremendous amount of overtime. The majority of the maintenance people that worked at my old plant make between seventy and ninety thousand dollars a year. Some have made as much as a hundred thousand dollars a year. That's spending a lot of time at the plant, folks, a lot of ten- and twelve-hour days and a lot of six- and seven-day workweeks.

They have worked this so long that their lifestyle is based on overtime. Now they need that overtime to maintain their much-improved lifestyles. We, as managers, made them that way. What is ironic is that at the same time we offer the overtime at some plants, we also hand off layoff slips at these same plants. It's really about greed. We have taught the people who have worked the overtime to get upset at the people who got laid off, because they are trying to get back into their plant for a job. The competition has actually gotten us to fight among ourselves! Another great tool in war games, because if there are two pipe fitters or millwrights or assemblers or clerks or whomever, instead of one, there will be less overtime. Management's position on this is that it is OK. If you lay people off, the benefits come out of a different pocket, and by working "less" people on "more" overtime you become more profitable. My belief is that the leaders, whether it's the country's leaders or the automotive industry's leaders, have missed the big picture. When everybody works . . . everybody buys!

I remember one time when the plumber came to my brother's shop to fix a broken water heater and the guy pulled up in a Toyota. Well, this guy barely made it to the door before big, I mean older, brother was on him like stink on shit. He told him that he would have to remove that truck from his place of business. He continued to tell him, "You see, I used to have a large crew of people working for me; now I only have a few and can barely keep them. The people that make that truck have almost put me out of business." Do you see how this works? Even the plumber lost a job, basically because of the truck he was driving. We must get back on track. We need to be loyal to "our" country and loyal to "our" companies, because on a clear day (no pun intended) we can hear them whispering, "Tora! Tora! Tora!"

In Toyota, they have always thought that "business is war." Well, they silently dug these trenches forty years ago, and because they have a great deal of patience and a belief in long-term progress, Pearl Harbor was nothing compared to what is about to happen. Our companies are not the only ones that are at fault here. Our government doesn't help the situation either. Due to the billions of dollars that Japan has poured into our country, they have become so strong that they are becoming the people in control. Yes, they are bringing in so much money now, it's become an addiction, not to drugs, but to power. Don't forget, I have said this over and over in this book: when you have the power, you will have the control. During this writing, General Motors ousted the chairman of the board and brought in a new "team" to run the company. Well, America has done the same thing, they ousted the old team and elected a new team and hope things will change. Remember that old saying: "What's good for General Motors is also good for America"? Let's bring it back. Make sure that the next new product you buy is made in America, but be careful now; make sure the company is owned by Americans. Ask the salesperson, even if you're standing in an American car showroom, where the car was built. If he supposedly doesn't know, go look on the window sticker; it's usually at the bottom of the window sticker. If the salesperson acts really stupid, make sure you point it out to him just before you leave that dealership. Because if he acts really stupid at this point of the game, you won't believe how stupid the dealership really is going to act after you buy that car and bring it back for service.

Prior to the election of President Clinton, our own government, who put a lot of dollars in their own pockets from foreign countries, was starting to get worried. I guess I shouldn't have said "prior to the new president," because during this writing NAFTA was passed. I can't believe the American public was deceived so badly, or should I say "so well"? I can't believe that "I" was deceived, as much as I was, by this guy from Arkansas. Along with many other millions of hardworking Americans, we were deceived by one of the best. I am glad to say that by the end of writing this book, America the Beautiful woke up and voted in a new Congress. Enough is enough. I can't wait until 1996. We are going in the right direction.

Well, back to the story in hand. Yes, now our own government is worried because the Japanese are building everything, not only cars, but computers and production machinery and many more items that are vital to our defense. They eventually are going to have the power to build the machinery that builds our defense equipment—yes, our defense equipment—because they will be the only companies left. The American people are starting to wake up. They don't like what is going on anymore; they don't like seeing the deterioration of our businesses, our economy, and, most of all, our country. A change is needed. They have finally realized that when there is only one company in town, you have no other place to go, and that is exactly what the Japanese are trying to work on. They are here, they have dug in, and they are inside the system, the American system. They are multiplying, and they are spreading like wildfire. They are buying so much property and so many companies, we eventually will rely on them to survive. A little added note here: When we talk about control and power, the Japanese have spent so much money in America and they have brought in so much of their own industry and bought up so much property, they now have the power and control to demand to pay low taxes on property and equipment and, believe it or not, some pay none. Just another edge they have on us, given to them by our "partners" in Washington. You know; they're the politicians with the well-lined pockets!

Every once in a while, I'll be talking to someone about his vacation in Hawaii and he will say, "You should see it now, everything is owned by the Japanese, but Martha and I had a good time," and then he goes on his merry way. Well, boys and girls, what about Montana? Yes, Montana. It seems the only way the Japanese can ship beef to their country without a lot of taxes or tariffs is for them to own their own ranches. So guess what? They are buying all the fucking ranches in Montana. You don't

153

have to fly twelve or fourteen hours to go to Montana like you do to Hawaii. Just go down the road a piece and make a left when you get to Wyoming. Come on . . . let's not lose our cowboys, too! Can you hear em? "yippie ki yae" and "howdy, partners" and "Tora! Tora! Tora!"

We just keep doing it to ourselves. Another quick example is the case of Universal Studios, now owned by the Japanese. Westinghouse and RCA both tried to buy the studios, but the government said they couldn't because it was a conflict of interest. But it's OK that one of Japan's largest and wealthiest companies can come right in and buy Universal up with hardly a question. The rules and regulations for European and Asian countries are extremely light for them to bring their products, money, and businesses into America. Now on the other hand, if we have American-made products that we sell in their countries, the rules and regulations for us are incredibly stiff. So the commanders (the American government) of the kamikaze pilots (yuppies and the other people that don't buy American-made products that are made in America BY AMERICAN COMPANIES) are the enemy within. SHHHH, I think I hear them. LISTEN: "Tora, Tora, Tora!"

Just a Thought

Pres. Bill Clinton and Congress's 1993 Christmas message to America after NAFTA was passed (what NAFTA really stands for to America's working class) is "NACHOS AND FRIJOLES TO ALL."

I think what Billy and the old Congress were really trying to say was that it won't be long before the working-class people that are left will be eating corn chips and beans after we lose our jobs to foreign countries.

19

Nice House—Nobody Home!

by Rino Pagnucco

As you can tell, I tend to do a lot of comparing. My biggest comparison, obviously, is General Motors and America. You know, in most cases, there are certain signals that in life are sent out to people to give them a chance to change before something good or bad happens. It's kind of like you know you eat the wrong foods and you eat too much of them and you really know the consequences, but do you stop? Hell, no! It's easier to say, "I'll exercise tomorrow, when I have time." There is always an excuse, and it doesn't have to be a good one either; any excuse will do. You'll make up some excuse that fits the reason why you should continue to eat that "eighth" piece of pizza or that second serving of deep-fried chicken wings dipped in thick bleu-cheese dressing. "Damn, you only go around once. I am not going to do what my doctor told me to do. Hell, it sounded like he said, 'If it tastes good, spit it out!' He only went to school for ten years and probably only saw hundreds of people, in the same situation, die from massive heart attacks caused from clogged arteries. I mean what the hell does he know?"

It's like that guy who invented the railroad crossing signals. Here is something that goes on and off and makes an annoying clanging sound, red flashers blink, and that usually only happens when a train is coming. It tells you to stop and not go over these tracks until the train has passed. All people have to do is follow the directions, but every year the death rate at railroad crossings goes up. Who really cares if the arm at the railroad crossing doesn't come down? You mean you can't tell from that irritating clanging noise and those red flashers that keep going on and off? And, most of all, unless you are blind, you can see this huge fucking piece of locomotion with a big bright light in the middle of it blowing its whistle frantically to tell you it's going to run your ass over if you get on those tracks. What other signals—or should I say how many signals?—do we need to get our attention?

While I'm on a roll here, let me give you another example. By now you also know I'm in and out of airports a lot. Well, when you are going to your gate there are these automated side-walks you can get on that take you down the aisle. They're like "flat" escalators. So tell me, why do they have this moving sidewalk divided into two halves? One half is for the people who are "still walking"! Now, this doesn't even begin to make sense. If you have to actually go out of your way to get on it, then why would you get on and continue to walk? These are the same people that are saying, "Excuse me; excuse me. I'm in a hurry!" but if they had just continued walking, they would have gotten to their destination sooner. I don't know; I just don't know.

One more quick example and then I will get on with this chapter. My partner and I have gone several times to Charlotte, North Carolina, in October for one of the Nascar races. It's the only Nascar race I attend. (I prefer Indy cars, but since A. J. Foyt retired I am going elsewhere.) OK, here's the picture. The race is called the "Mellow Yellow 500." The "Mellow Yellow 500" race car is a Pontiac. This Pontiac has "Mellow Yellow" written all over it. It is the "Mellow Yellow" race car. There is a tremen-dous amount of advertising prior to the race that depicts Kyle Petty, the driver; Mellow Yellow, the soft drink; and Pontiac, the car. You would think that the pace car for the race would be a

Pontiac. Well, it's not; it's an Oldsmobile. Don't ask; I don't know.

At the same race, I went down to the gift area and tried to buy a commercial coffee mug featuring the "Mellow Yellow 500." I couldn't. They were only selling coffee mugs featuring the "Coca Cola 600" race, which is held every May. Why isn't the race car a Pontiac? Why can't I get a "Mellow Yellow 500" coffee mug? Because their thinking is just like GM thinking. The people at the Charlotte Speedway think that the people that come to buy that stuff will buy it no matter what it is. Well, you'd better wake up. You see, the General thought the same way. Market shares continue to keep slipping away, but no real changes are being made. The body styles on some cars have been basically the same for the past seventeen years. Take a look at GM vans and Suburbans. The thinking here is: *It's a GM product; they'll buy it.* You know that train we were talking about earlier? Well, it's getting closer and closer to the railroad crossing, and not only the General is edging out into the path of it, but many of today's businesses are also going in that direction. Why can't we see the signals? The new top brass at General Motors can't figure it out. They continue to ask themselves, "Why isn't it coming together?"

Well, let me tell you again and again. It's the "thinking process" and the "work philosophy" that have to change. The thinking process and work philosophy haven't changed in thirty years. If you were to walk into the GM Building in Detroit, you would think that you were going back in time. This is a building that is supposed to represent smart, authoritative business decisions. The facade is almost impressive. Then you just happen to notice that this building has an air conditioner in every other window! The executives are dressed the same way the executives were dressed in 1959. Some of those executives from 1959 are still there, and so is their way of thinking. The real problem is . . . these are the people that are still in charge. They hate it when they hear that their thinking needs to be "Saturnized." They not only need to teach this thing called "TEAM CONCEPT," but they also need to "implement" it. They teach it in every GM plant in the country. They start right there in making sure the hourly people are trained, except they don't teach themselves. They talk it, but they don't walk it. You can't expect the people that work for you to perform according to this concept if you can't do it at the top. No matter how much they reengineer the product and no matter how many people we lay off or retire early, we still won't change the outcome of a business that continues to lose market shares unless we change the "thinking" and the "philosophy" of everyone. Not only does this have to be done, but it has to be done "yesterday."

Here's an example. The Pontiac Grand Prix and the Chevrolet Lumina, at the time of this writing, weren't selling as well as they should have been. Nice cars, they ran well, but they had no airbags. No matter what your opinion is on safety items, they are a major selling point to many buyers in today's market, especially moms. Chrysler and Ford immediately got on this bandwagon, making airbags a major feature in the selling of their cars. Chrysler was first in their advertising of airbags, and they took major-market-share customers away from everyone else. Bottom line: their sales were up. So were Ford's. Ford realized this was a problem on one of their car lines and actually stopped production of the vehicle. They brought everyone down to the production lines, from engineers to maintenance coordinators, and redesigned the vehicle and the tooling involved to make this safety change. Even though it cost a tremendous amount of money to do this, they gave the public what they wanted and were able to continue to keep and possibly gain market share, never losing sight of the reason that we are in the business is to sell cars!

GM sales were slumping. Pontiac and Chevrolet knew the problem existed and, because of the existing 1959 style of management and the multiple layers of committee bargaining, said it would take two to three years to get the airbags into their Grand Prix, Lumina, and other model lines. Not just one model year to turn it around, but two to three model years. It's because that "old" style of thinking and philosophy takes that long to process and approve changes. It's about one committee meeting with another committee, and let's not forget the other committee; we wouldn't want to hurt their feelings. By the time everybody met with everybody, we lost the war. How much more of the market share did we lose while all these meetings were going on?

How many car sales have we lost because many customers now like the competition's product better than ours? Have we lost these customers for good? I think that train is close enough now; why don't we just pull out in front of it.

One time when I was in Miami, Florida, there was a warning that a hurricane was coming and we had better get ready. Well, some people got ready alright; they got ready for a "beach party." A hurricane beach party, so to speak. These people were going to get "blown" away, one way or another. What causes this type of thinking? It's no different than crossing the train tracks when there is a train coming, I guess. It's obvious to me that there are many people that just keep saying, "It's not going to happen to me. It's not going to happen to us." Unfortunately, some of these people are in the decision making process that affects so many others.

It's about reality. In General Motors' case, just because something was good in 1959 and 1969 doesn't mean it's still OK today. Too many things have changed. If the world is changing in "their" thinking and you're the only one that isn't chang-ing . . . hang on to your ass, because you're about to lose it. We can't forget that we are not only in the automobile business; we are also in the people business. If we say we are making changes, but these changes are more layoffs, plant closings, and early re-tirements, because that's what is going to make it better, our old style of thinking is kicking in. If we keep building more plants outside the United States (we now have approximately twenty-seven in Mexico alone, not including Eastern Europe, Russia, China, and Korea), who the hell is going to buy the cars that they build? Americans will be out of jobs. I guess they think the Mexicans, the Eastern Europeans, the Russians, or maybe the Chinese or Koreans will buy them. If I recall properly, you went to these countries because the help is "mucho cheaper," but the price of the cars didn't get any cheaper. Don't forget, we lost our jobs; we can't buy these products anymore either. Wake up! Who the hell is going to buy the cars?

America, believe it or not, revolves around the automobile industry. When our industry is down, normally the economy as a whole is poor. The auto industry affects everything. It's the difference between buying a new house or just putting an addition onto the one you already have. When you lay off an autoworker it normally affects seven jobs throughout the community. Just ask around. It ain't what it used to be; the opportunities aren't there anymore. The millionaires aren't letting anybody else in their circle anymore. There was a time, not too long ago, that when you had a million dollars, you were considered a millionaire. Now economists say in order to be a millionaire in today's world, you must have $50 million. When the news media says unemployment is down, it usually means those unemployed fourteen-dollar-an-hour autoworkers who were laid off ran out of unemployment benefits and are now working for six to eight dollars an hour, some less. Not only does General Motors have to change their way of thinking; so do we, the people. We must stop buying all cars that are not made in America by American companies. That includes the cars made by General Motors, Ford, and Chrysler that are "NOT" made in America. We must absolutely, positively stop buying foreign cars. Bring those jobs back here. When you buy that Japanese or any other foreign car, the dollar goes to Japan or whatever other country first and whatever pennies are left over are then brought back to America. When you buy that American car that's made in America, the buck starts and stops in the USA. In order to do this, General Motors must give the customers what "they" want, not what General Motors wants. QUALITY must be FIRST.

Losing market shares every year is just another signal that should tell someone something is very, very, very wrong. We are not listening to the people in America, because the signal that they are sending back to us is that they are "NOT" buying our cars. They aren't discriminating between the cheaper cars and the expensive cars either. They're tired of bringing a new car back to the dealership over and over again for repairs. They're tired of losing a day's pay while their new car is being worked on. Many times there are no loaners, even if you were so promised. The dealerships think they are doing you a favor by giving you a subcompact car while you are paying for a full-size car that doesn't work. Even worse, you have to make an appointment with the dealership for next week for a car that doesn't work today. Well, it must be time to drive in front of that train, because all the signals are working. Read the signals and obey the rules. Common sense, basic simple shit. Why doesn't someone ask Sears and Kmart how much of their business they have lost to Wal-Mart or Sam's Club or Target? Why don't we ask IBM how much of their business Apple and Compac have taken away from them? Doesn't anybody read the signals until it's too late? It can't happen to us—we're General Motors; we're America. Nice house—nobody home!

20

The Great American Automobile Tragedy

by Rino Pagnucco

We lose a little on every car, but we make up for it in volume!
—GM executive statement to the press, 1993

During the summer of 1992, I couldn't help comparing the U.S. economy and the way America has been perceived as no longer being the world's greatest nation with the way General Motors is no longer being perceived as the greatest automobile company in the world. Former president Bush was perceived as spending so much time doing business in and for other countries that he forgot about his own. Well, I see the similarities between governmental practice and GM procedures. General Motors was spending so much time and effort closing plants in America and opening new ones overseas, they forgot who buys American automobiles. They seem to have forgotten that the men and women who build their products also buy their products. For some stupid fucking reason, they don't seem to understand that when you move these plants out of America you're also moving jobs out of America. The automotive industry runs the economy of America and the world. It's very simple. No matter what country we talk about, when the automotive industry is growing and is productive, so is the economy. When the automotive industry goes sour, people stop buying. They not only stop buying cars; they stop buying everything. Is this so hard to see? They stop shopping for that new bigger house they were going to buy and consider possibly putting an addition onto their old house or doing nothing at all. They don't buy a new car; they fix the one they have. They don't buy a new second car, they buy a used second car, and it goes on and on and on. Why is it that a high percentage of our children won't make as much as their parents? Why is it that the unemployment line has more college graduates in it than ever before?

On Sunday, November 17, 1991, *The Detroit News* published an article titled "An American Tragedy," by Deb Price and Richard Ryan. They said: "There are serious things going on in the workplace that pit people against each other at times when they should be cooperating." The demands are up, and the satisfaction is down. Symptoms include ulcers, depression, tragedies—such as the Royal Oak, Michigan, post office shooting that left five people dead. Growing global competition, an era of mergers and downsizing, and the rapid introduction of new technology have made workplaces remarkably different and more stressful than a decade ago. The way supervisors treat people can cause stress, and that can cause pain. The production is supposed to be up, and the number of people to fulfill that production is down. Previously, employees felt jobs were secure, wages would increase, and benefits would rise. Employers would retain workers during bad times, because of the confidence of good times returning. But due to the foreign competition, a decline in the economic growth, and demands by shareholders, a sense of job security has declined. Companies responded to the new pressure by becoming lean and mean. And, for the first time, management began to experience the job insecurity once felt only by the rank and file.

Jobs are less rewarding today. People don't feel there is a long-term commitment from their employer. Computerization is

163

making tremendous demands on workers and managers. It's a new form of work, and not everyone can make that changeover well.

During the Great Depression changing jobs was viewed as a great risk. Changing jobs is now considered the only way to advance. Stay in one job too long, and people begin to look at you strangely. Trust levels zero out when you get comfortable with people and then they're moved. If you are growing in the organization or in the department you are working in and you know what the problems are, it is here and now that these problems should be addressed so the new system can work and everyone will benefit from it. Well, that's not the way the system works. Typically, General Motors' way is to change the person, not the problem. General Motors now says it needs to have an aggressive management approach. They have finally gotten into the Japanese way of thinking. Toyota's objective is not only to win, but to drive the competition out of business. Now that's aggressive. This was General Motors when it was at its apex. Remember when they were wealthy, confident, and innovative? We were proud, we had principles, and we were loyal. In 1955, General Motors had 50 percent of the market. In the March 1992 issue of *Reader's Digest* an article titled "On History Lessons" stated that according to an edition of *Business Week* published in 1958, an executive made this comment: "With over 50 foreign cars already on sale here the Japanese auto industry isn't likely to carve out a big slice of the U.S. market." Seventeen layers of management were between the chairman and the assembly workers. Executives lost sight of building cars. Many of the salary and hourly workforce at General Motors sometimes wonder if the General really wants to be in the automobile building business anymore. They have lost all sight of the real reason why they are General Motors. Japan, Germany, and other foreign countries were designing small cars. This is where the executives failed to ask the workers how to improve cars and jobs. The reward was in company loyalty (better known as the "BUDDY SYSTEM"), not in initiative. General Motors has now become very competitive. In order to compete in today's marketplace, with some very tough competition, they are going to have to get synchronized. They are going to have to use team concept and, above all, change their 1959 style of thinking to enter today's business world. They must change. We need to know the difference and separate the past "GOOD" practices and remove and stop allowing the "BAD" practices to continue. One of the bad practices I am talking about is the hiring back of the 1959 style of management "BUDDIES" (after they have retired) as "CONSULTANTS."

In 1987, I started teaching team concept, at least what was perceived to be team concept. In 1989, I quit teaching it. Not because it wasn't the right thing to do, but because it wasn't happening the way they said it was going to happen. Higher management in the plants kept telling Roger Smith and Bob Stemple that everything was fine, and it really wasn't. According to the May 4, 1992 issue of *Fortune Magazine*, Sam Walton (billionaire boy scout of Bentonville, Arkansas) built an empire on a belief in value. He pioneered ideals like impairment to cripple the competition. He stressed flexibility and action over deliberation, sharing information and profits with employees, lowering the cost to the customers . . . CUSTOMER-DRIVEN SERVICE. Nothing happens until a customer walks into a store with a purpose, buys something, and walks out. Everyone's ideas count. American people want value.

The truth about American workers is that the men and women who run the factories and staff the offices do surprisingly well in the global competitive race . . . but only when managers give them a chance. A defective workforce can cause erosion. Investing in a new plant and new equipment isn't enough. Let's not only use their hands; let's use their minds.

Let me say something here about "SHOP or FACTORY RATS," as they were once called. I am proud to tell you I know

165

these people. I grew up with them, and I was one. If you didn't actually see these people working in the factory, you would probably never guess that's where they worked. See, at one time, "FACTORY RATS" were looked down upon. Now we wish that our sons and daughters, with four to six years of college, could make that kind of money or even get that kind of job. These same shop and factory rats of old are now the strongest defenders of our economy. Thank you, Mr. and Mrs. Shop Rat, for hanging in there.

In July 1992, at the Democratic Convention, one of the world's greatest speakers of all time, New York's governor Mario Cuomo, stated, "The Ship of State is headed for the rocks. The crew knows it; the passengers know it. Only the captain of the ship appears not to know it." When I heard this, I said to myself, *My god, this is exactly what is happening to General Motors.* This is what I have been trying to lead up to, as I stated in the beginning of this chapter. How ironic that the government and General Motors run very similarly in almost every way. I can see how they are related. Politicians, lying to their bosses, saying everything is alright and just because we are America everything is going to be OK, it will come back on its own. Likewise, because we are General Motors we are going to stay on top. As I stated before, just like the politicians, General Motors forgot about its own country.

The new president, who so well deceived us in the beginning, has just "bought off Congress" to pass NAFTA. What a shame. If we give up just one job to another country, we have given up one too many! Let me make this clear, I don't mind helping other countries, but we need to take care of our own first! Just in case you forgot, Billy, America is our country. You know what's really funny? The only people that normally say, "Money isn't everything," are the people who have a lot of money. And to the people who have money . . . money isn't the problem. One of the only divisions in General Motors that was making money was their overseas operations. So, I guess the thinking here is if you close enough plants in America and open new ones in other countries, this will make more profits, right? Well, in both politics and General Motors, I wish someone would wake the fuck up and smell the roses, because they're dying.

It's not only General Motors; it's everyone. Let's call it . . . the unfair advantage. But why do we allow it? We allow car dealerships that made money from General Motors in the "GOOD TIMES" to buy a Honda, Toyota, or Lexus dealership, and then they cry about how General Motors is screwing them as they get into their helicopter to go to their oceanfront property, yacht, or condo in Hawaii, which General Motors paid for. This also happens at Ford and Chrysler.

Did you know that only 10 percent of the people that come into a dealership leave because of the product? That really means that the American people build a damn good product. So what makes the other 90 percent leave? Half the battle is to get the customer into your store. Once he is there, it is up to the people in the store to sell themselves. Yes . . . themselves. I mean you, the customer, already like the product; otherwise you wouldn't be there. Well, about another 15 percent will usually leave after getting some facts together, because they need additional time to check out their budget. About 5 percent are the wisest of all, because they are the comparison shoppers. If you were to ask any financial adviser today, "What's the worst financial deal you can make today?" he would probably answer, "Buying a new car." So, what the smart comparison shopper is really doing is shopping for the best/worst deal. Again, let's compare the automobile industry with the government. Remember, I said they go hand in hand. Remember when we voted for a new president in 1992? Of the two candidates . . . neither one was very good, but we had to choose the best or better of the worst. So, go buy a new car without shopping around. It's a matter of how much do you want to lose? As far as the new president goes, I think the "WORKING PEOPLE" of America better hang onto their ass.

Let's get back to the comparison shoppers. They're shopping for the best financial deal and the best service. If you accept the first deal the dealer gives you, you are doing an injustice to your wallet.

Here is how dealers do it to themselves. They allow about 70 percent of the people to leave because of mistreatment. As a customer, you were treated poorly or rudely or the salesperson acted like he thought you owed him something for coming in. Next case, when you brought your car in for service and went to pick it up, it wasn't done because they didn't have the part and, of course, you will have to bring it back in . . . another time. I can't tell you how many times I have been in dealerships with customers waiting for a salesperson and there wasn't anyone available in the showroom. This especially happens to women. This I can't figure out. Women usually make the major decision on car buying. I mean they usually are in charge of the budget; they have a major say about the color. They are part of the decision making process in the family and, in most cases, also are part of the money making process. So tell me, why do we treat women like they are nobody? It's even worse when they have to bring the car in for service. There was one time when I was in New York working in a dealership and this lady came into an empty showroom. There were no customers except for her. It was early in the morning and there were three salespeople on the floor, but nobody was waiting on her. I went over to her and introduced myself as an employee of Pontiac Motor Division, not of the dealership, but could I help by getting someone to help her? She said she was looking for a car but really wanted to see how long it took for someone to help her, because she was a woman. She walked out. Sometimes we just do it to ourselves.

On numerous occasions, I have had to call the dealership to get someone to help a customer get something fixed or adjusted when all the time the dealership could have corrected the problem from the beginning. You know the concept: correct the problem, without outside intervention, create an atmosphere of goodwill, and save the customer a lot of aggravation. Sometimes, we just do it to ourselves. Now let me tell you, all these divisions have a customer-assistance telephone number. If you are a customer and you feel you have been mistreated, for whatever reason, don't hesitate to call that 1-800 number. If you, as a customer, have to pick up the phone and dial that number, it's too late. The dealership, in my opinion, has failed to gain your confidence and now faces a good possibility of losing you as a return customer. In addition, the dealership is also about to receive some very unfavorable word-of-mouth advertising. We all know that the best or worst kind of advertising is word of mouth. Sometimes we just do it to ourselves.

I remember another time when I had to call the general sales manager of a dealership in Detroit to ask him if any of his salespeople were driving Pontiac Bonnevilles that the dealership had supplied them with. He responded, "Yes." I quickly asked him why one of his customers who has had to bring back his $20,000 Bonneville for repair over a half a dozen times, leaving it there two to three days or sometimes a week at a time, received in return a Sunbird to drive? Not only is the customer unhappy, because they can't fix his car, but he is paying for a $20,000 car and driving a $12,000 car. The general sales manager rudely replied, "Well, you don't expect me to pull one of my salespeople out of his car, do you?" I just couldn't believe what I was hearing. I had to remind this overpaid dickhead just what those dealer company cars were for. In conclusion, the customer received a loaner vehicle that equaled the type of car that he brought in for service. Sometimes we just do it to ourselves. Well, I won the battle, but we lost the customer.

The competition is going out of their way to satisfy customers. The way we treat them, it won't take much to get them on the competition's side. For example, in Japan if you were a customer that walked into a store and asked for a product that you wanted but did not see, management would send people looking for it or give you a promise that they would deliver it to your home, even if it cost them more to find it and they had to take a small loss on the sale. What I'm trying to say here is that at least they would make an attempt at satisfying the customer. Getting the customer in your store, whether it's a candy store or a dealership, is the largest part of the battle. To allow a customer to leave emptyhanded or in disgust is just plain bad business. To allow our repeat customers to leave in disgust is a damn shame. In America, we have become very complacent. If we go into a department store and ask the clerk (if we can find a clerk) for a certain item that we can't find, he might say, "Nope, we're out of it. Come back next Saturday," or worse, he will say, "Sorry, we are out right now, but if you go next door to our competitors they might have it." Well, why don't they just get a razor blade and cut their wrists? When we go to buy a car we do the same thing. What if I told you that some of the competition (let's just call them those foreign people) when it comes to servicing their product at times will deliver an equal type of car to your house, pick up your troubled car and take it back to the dealership, then call you when your car is ready, and I mean completed and ready? Let me tell you, I am not making this up. We are doing it to ourselves. We expect people to come into our stores just because we're General Motors or Ford, Kmart, Sears, or IBM. The companies like Honda, Toyota, Saturn, Meijer Thrifty Acres, and Wal-Mart have taken a large share of the customers away from the others, because they were able to see that customers were willing to change. Dissatisfied customers who were being treated like this is the only game in town, take it or leave it, just ain't taking it no more. They're leaving it.

In July of 1992, *The Detroit News* printed that Chevrolet Division was upset over the fact that the Saturn Corporation was selling more cars than they were. Saturn has built-in both quality and customer satisfaction in their factory and also in their showrooms. I know this sounds corny, but we have to get back into ourselves. We have to treat people like we want to be treated. I don't want to go to three stores for an item I am looking for. I don't want to go to a store that just advertised a product on sale and when I get there they are out of the product! I want to go to one store. I want to build a quality "anything" the way it should work. I want to take away all the excuses from the dealerships and the factories on why it wasn't fixed and built right the first time. Before I get off my soap box, this is not only a message to management, but to everyone . . . we have to start treating everyone that we come into contact with as our "customer." This means the person we just left and the person we are about to meet. It doesn't make any difference whether you are the CEO of the company or the return bottle person. . . . Treat the customer like you want to be treated.

This following bit of information was hanging on a dealership wall. Unfortunately, it was in a back room, hanging where no one could see it:

YOU OFTEN HEAR THAT
"QUALITY IS EVERYBODY'S JOB"
AND THAT'S TRUE,
BUT IT MUST START WITH MANAGEMENT.
MANAGEMENT'S JOB IS TO LEAD PEOPLE TOWARD A
GOAL.
AND QUALITY IS THE ONLY GOAL THAT MATTERS.
YOUR CUSTOMERS
ARE IN A PERFECT POSITION
TO TELL YOU ABOUT QUALITY, BECAUSE
THAT'S ALL THEY ARE REALLY BUYING.
THEY'RE NOT BUYING A PRODUCT.
THEY'RE BUYING YOUR ASSURANCE

171

THAT THEIR EXPECTATIONS
FOR THAT PRODUCT
WILL BE MET.
AND YOU HAVEN'T REALLY GOT
ANYTHING ELSE TO SELL BUT THOSE ASSURANCES.
YOU HAVEN'T REALLY GOT
ANYTHING ELSE TO SELL
BUT
QUALITY.

—John Guaspari
"I KNOW IT WHEN I SEE IT"

21

Get More Toilet Paper

by Rino Pagnucco

More headlines from the wonderful world of General Motors. In the September 1992 issue of *Inside General Motors*, vice president of personnel for North America Gerald Knechtel said that "General Motor's leadership remains committed to employees and retirees," and, "we want to retain quality health care programs and still ensure General Motor's future success." Well, I'll be dipped in horse shit and rolled in cracker meal, not two days later, on September 18, 1992, Robert Stempel, chairman of the board, delivered a satellite message to all of his GM employees and retirees on how they would have to now start paying more, much more, on their health care co-payments and deductibles. Boy, just when you would think that the top dogs at General Motors are talking to each other, they continue making believers out of us that the right hand doesn't know what the left hand is doing. Folks, it gets worse. Another vice president of corporate personnel, Richard O'Brien, and his buddy, Gerald Knechtel, both say that GM health care costs have contributed to General Motors' declining competitiveness in the marketplace. Transplant automakers have three major advantages over General Motors in the areas of health care: a younger workforce, fewer retirees, and fewer health plans.

Every time the top officials at General Motors mess with the retirees, they lose. It's only fair that they lose. General Motors negotiated an agreement with their employees that states: "This is how much money you are going to receive when you retire. These figures include your benefits and pension, so plan the rest of your retirement life around these figures." Most of the retirees do this. So, when the retirees did make their decisions, based on the figures that they were given in good faith, General Motors turns around whenever they damn well feel like it and say, "Times are tough. Please excuse us for mismanaging the business, but we are taking some money back from you." It is unfair of General Motors to say, "We are going to give you this much money to live on the rest of your life," and then deviate from the preplanned figures at any time they wish. I would like to see them go to Roger Smith and say, "Oh, by the way, Rog, we know it's hard being retired on $2,500 a week, but we need to take some back." I can hear that squeaky fucking laugh now. Do you think Bob Stempel, who made over $5,000 a week when he was the chairman of the board, knows what effect this has on someone who is on a fixed income? By the time the retirees get into court and they get everything settled, General Motors (knowing that they are going to court and that they are going to lose) will still have saved millions of dollars. Brilliant!

General Motors is now grasping for every "excuse" they can possibly get their hands on so they can tell the public why they are not regaining any of the market share. When the top executives can't commit to and have team concept among themselves but expect everyone else to, they are going to make excuses and not solutions. From the people on the inside it sure looked like the corporation was setting up a game plan for the 1993 UAW negotiations, using the salary employees and the retirees as pawns.

As far as those transplant autoworkers having younger employees and fewer retirees, we just do it to ourselves. How many contract people do you think General Motors has? By contract people, I mean people who retire from General Motors or another company on Friday and return to work for General Motors on Monday. It also can be someone young and experienced at some particular skill that a certain department can't get done with the people they have, so they hire a contract person. Contract people get no benefits, and the head count doesn't show any increase. Now, you have a contract person. The answer is approximately 18 percent. So how does this sound? Eighteen percent of the people that represent General Motors don't really work for General Motors. Some of these people never cleaned out their desk. It's about head count. This may sound confusing, but this is how it works. Higher management tells middle management that they have to reduce the amount of people in their workforce or department by 10 percent. So, if you have thirty people working for you, you have to get rid of three people. Transfer one person, force two to retire, and promise one of them that you will hire him back as a "contract person." In most cases, such as the retreads, as they are so often referred to by the audit staff, they have to work at least twenty weeks out of the year. Now, these contract people are no longer on the head count. You now have twenty-seven people on your rolls. Don't worry about that twenty-eighth person sitting there collecting not only his retirement, but also a new salary for contract work. In the area where I last worked there were eleven retirees. They called them retreads. Let me shock you a little more. They get $200 a day, plus all expenses. They get $26 to $34 a day for meals (depending on what city they are in), plus (yes, there's more) hotel accommodations, plus airfare. Now include their retirement pay, because they are still getting paid for being retired, and total up that General Motors is really shelling out around $8,000 to $10,000 a month per each person who in management's eyes isn't really there.

The retreads in the audit staff are only one example of what I consider excessive spending. Included also are the people that the General subcontracts as full-time employees, but they are not really on the rolls. They have to pay another company, like a company called SUB CORE (based in Warren, Michigan), which these contract people actually work for. Some contract people are also called consultants. Some of these so-called consultants were ex-managers who retired with a special early retirement package; plus they receive a consultant salary as high as $1,500 a week. One guy told me he had heard of an ex–GMC truck manager that retired and then was rehired as a consultant to dealers at a figure of $9,000 a month, plus he still got his retirement pay. This is a perfect example of the "BUDDY SYSTEM." I have no way to prove these last two figures other than common knowledge. But from what I have seen, the way General Motors seems to think there is a bottomless pit of money, I just have to believe they are true. It is my understanding that the plan within General Motors is to add even more contract help. There are hundreds of retirees that are employed as contract workers in General Motors.

WHO THE FUCK ARE WE KIDDING HERE? We are spending a lot of money out of one pocket and saying we are saving it in another. You can understand why they can't figure out why they are losing their ass.

We have a fine, young workforce that is ready and willing to do a good job for us. Instead, we're not hiring or even retaining the ones we already have. We are laying off and letting go the ones in whom we already have invested a great deal of money and time. Why? Well, those people who aren't really there (the contract people) have their jobs, that's why. Division and department heads can show their bosses that their head count is down. So, the bottom line is that we're not training our future workforce to make the system better. We are just pissing on little brush fires, and the whole fucking forest is burning! It is General Motors' continuation of its 1959 style of thinking, which is the same in their dealership showrooms as it is in their corporate offices: "We are General Motors and if you don't like what we have to offer, you can just leave.''

We have not only lost many great young minds, but some truly great older minds and, from the looks of our market share, many a customer! Just how much of the market share must we lose before we realize that these so-called consultants who we have rehired who, in many cases, couldn't do the job when they really worked for us are in the position to tell us ''again'' how to run or—should I say ''RUIN''?—our current business.

22

When the Shit Hits the Fan

by Rino Pagnucco

While writing this book, I didn't think General Motors had the balls to pick up the shovel and shovel the proverbial shit into the fan. On October 26, 1992, the newly assigned board of directors pressured the chairman of the board, Robert Stempel, to resign. When General Motors announces to the world that you, as an employee of the largest automobile manufacturer in the world (at that time), have decided to resign, in reality they are saying, "Bobby, yo, Bobby, You can go public and say you can't go on due to health reasons and you are going to resign. Or we can go to the press and say, 'Since Bob can't seem to get his shit together, we have decided to fire him.' We would like to send this message out to everyone here at the corporation and let you know that no one, and we mean NO ONE, is too big for us to fuck with! Now, Mr. Auto Executive, how would you like to go out?"

This was the start or the beginning of the end, depending on how you looked at it. It was the end of the old regime and the beginning of the new. Effective November 2, 1992, John G. Smale, former Procter & Gamble executive, was now the new chairman of the board and John "Jack" Smith was now the new chief executive officer and president. The boardroom shakeup that put a new team in charge of General Motors was only the start of many new changes to come. Five new and younger members replaced seven older members.

Ironically, on November 3, 1992, America itself was changing. America voted for a new president. Once again, a new and younger group coming in to run a different kind of business, the business of the country. It just goes to show that the people at General Motors and the people in the country were waiting for somebody—in these cases it was Robert Stempel and President Bush—to do something with the ongoing problems of both the business and the country, and nothing was happening. Everyone at the top, both at General Motors and in America, thought that everything would be alright all by itself! With time, everything would turn around by itself and everything would be just "PEACHY." Why? Why were these two leaders (Stempel and Bush) so surprised when they were standing in front of the fan and the shit was all over their faces? This just went to show everyone, whether it was the top job at a large corporation or the top job in the country, that no matter what rung you are standing at on the ladder, you will still have to report to the people sometime. This is just a higher level of "INTIMIDATION 101." It's about million-dollar salaries, instead of thousand-dollar or hundred-dollar salaries. It's also about taking action. It reminds me of when a doctor has to make a decision to amputate an arm or leg to save the rest of the body. The body has to start over and relearn reaching or walking skills. Not to do anything would be the worst thing a person could do. This is exactly what happened at General Motors under Stempel and America under President Bush. Bottom line: they both lost their jobs.

I guess my partner and I are kind of like Perot in the presidential race of 1992. What do we have to lose by telling the truth? We felt we had to do something in writing this book because we still love General Motors. We want to see Americans buy American products, made in America, but we also want to see a "better" American product made. Not only in General Motors, but everywhere in America. We have the people to do it; we have the technology to do it; we now need the leaders to do it! If you are going to shut down a plant and put thousands of people in America out of work, then shut it down and reopen a new one in America to implement the new and better ideas that you want implemented. Why should we give up "OUR" jobs to someone else? Are the "SAME" leaders that led "US" to where we are today going to lead "THEM" (whatever country they may be) any better?

We must STOP sending jobs to Mexico and other foreign countries only because its cheaper. We want to get it back; we want to see the mark of excellence when we see that "Made in America" label.

23

Eighty Years of Henry Ford

by Rino Pagnucco

So there I was, in June of 1993, sitting in another hotel room waiting for my two-hundred-and-fifty-some days to pass by so I could retire and there is this television show that came on in the morning, you know, one of those *Good Morning America* or *Good Morning Today* or *Good Morning* shows, and it was about a man named Henry Ford and the Henry Ford Museum, and can you guess where? Yes, sir, in Dearborn, Michigan. They were talking about how brilliant Henry Ford was and how gutsy he was in some of the decisions that he made. Even eighty years later, one of those decisions still holds true.

In 1914, there were very few jobs and money was tight, similar to the economy of today. The Ford Motor Company was only selling cars to the people who already had money. The automobile was either a luxury item or a novelty. Henry decided to take a chance; he was going to take a chance on people. He was going to give everyone that worked for him a raise. Not a large raise, but a raise. He decided to shorten the workday from the normal twelve hours down to ten. Then, to top it off, he hired more people, almost double the amount he already had. At this point, everyone thought he finally had gone completely off his rocker. His theory behind this was that he could sell more cars if he could sell them to the people that worked for him. The more people that worked for him, the more cars he sold. He kept the cars affordable, so he would sell even more. His sales almost doubled; production soared by selling to the people that worked for him. What a great idea!

Something else happened. Henry inadvertently caused the economy of the nation to become better. More jobs, more money. Housing increased; steel production increased. Not only could the factory worker afford the car that Henry made, but now he could afford a better house to live in and maybe some other luxuries, like sewing machines and so many other things that put so many other people to work. The domino effect of the automobile industry had started to take off. The automobile was not a luxury item anymore; it was a necessity.

Eighty years have passed and, unfortunately, the theory that Henry Ford once had, at least in General Motors, has become just the opposite. The decisions have been made to close the plants, lay off the workers, alienate the workers that you still have by taking benefits away from them. Let's build and open new plants in other countries. Let's take Henry Ford's idea of prosperity and run it backward. Do we really need to do this? How can we sit here and wonder why we aren't selling cars like we used to? How can we wonder why unemployment is so high, housing is down, small businesses are going out of business? We opened a lot of plants in other countries. Are they buying the ''American-made'' cars produced in their countries? We are on a collision course going back into time. It's simply bad management decisions that higher management hasn't learned to step up to. The 1959 style of management is still there. Excessive spending and poor management decisions are still General Motors' major problem. We haven't learned anything in eighty years!

Our Philosophy (The Plan)

Plan your work;
Work your plan.
Fail to plan;
Plan to fail.

24

What Not to Buy

by Rino Pagnucco

So, you ask yourself, "What should I NOT buy to help America get back to where it should be?" Don't buy anything that is not made in America, by Americans, and owned by an American-owned company. It's that simple! We must understand that it is very important that it must be an American-owned company. What people don't understand is that companies like Honda of Ohio, Toyota of Kentucky, Merecedes-Benz of Alabama, and all the other foreign car manufacturers that are building automobile factories in the United States (and manufacturers of other products that are being brought over here and built here) are actually deceiving us by putting us to work. Every dollar that is spent on their product goes immediately to their country and then gets divided up and goes into the proper places, first and foremost, in that country. Whatever is left over comes back to America. America is the last place the "change" goes to. Beware; it's part of the "War Games."

The erosion has set in so much that it is obvious that there are some products that are no longer built in America and you have no choice but to buy that product from another country. We also do a good job of deceiving ourselves. Our management, for greed's sake, has done a wonderful job of doing the same thing. We build so-called American cars and we build them on foreign soil, putting more Americans out of work. The only people that are becoming wealthy here, folks, are the people on top. Top management, top executives, and top politicians. Their salaries get bigger and bigger every year, their bonuses get bigger and bigger (with better "deals" in the bad years) every year, and they are very well taken care of after they give up their positions.

Please, please, please make sure the products you are buying, from now on, are MADE IN AMERICA, BY AMERICANS AND AMERICAN-OWNED COMPANIES.

According to the *1993 General Motors Product Guide Booklet*, copyrighted by General Motors Corporation, here are some interesting facts about some of their cars and trucks and where they are built.

Car Line	Country Built
Chevrolet Lumina	Canada
Chevrolet full-size sport van	USA and Canada
Chevrolet full-size C/K pickup	USA and Canada
Chevrolet Geo Metro	Canada and Japan
Chevrolet Nova	Joint venture with Toyota
Chevrolet Geo Storm	Japan
Chevrolet Geo Tracker	Canada
Pontiac Lemans	Korea
Buick Century	USA and Mexico
Buick Regal	Canada
GMC Truck Rally/Ventura van	USA and Canada
GMC Truck Sierra pickup and crew cab	USA and Canada
GMC motor home chassis	USA and Canada

If you think Ford and Chrysler are any different, you are sadly mistaken. I called a Chrysler dealership, in the "Downriver Area" of Detroit, and told the new-car salesman that I was looking for a new car, but it had to be made in America. This snobby son of a bitch told me "I" was going to have to change my way of thinking, that there was no such thing as a completely American-made car. He was laughing. I sincerely hope that this guy loses his job first. I did find out that prior to 1994, most of the new car lines that Chrysler built, such as the Intrepid, Concord, and New Yorker, were built in Canada. They have been so successful with these new models since 1994 they were also starting to build some of them in America. All the "specialty" vehicles, such as the Dodge Viper and the Plymouth Prawler, are assembled here in America. Well, if we are good enough to build the "specialty vehicles," why aren't we good enough to build the others? Aren't we special? Here is a little something you should remember when you go looking for a new or used car that will help you know where the car was built. General Motors and Chrysler and most Fords use the same number system on their vehicle identification number (the VIN). If the VIN starts with the number one, it means that the vehicle was made somewhere in America. If it starts with any other number but one, it was made in another country.

I don't know what to say about joint ventures either. To me, they are just as bad. The Ford Probe, joint venture with Mazda; the minivan Mercury Villager, joint venture with Nissan; it just goes on and on and on. We have lost too many damn jobs to foreign countries and we just keep doing it to ourselves. Again, only because I am an equal opportunity writer, below this paragraph is a list of Ford and Chrysler products and where they are built. So when you do decide to go and buy or lease a new or used car, I'll say it again and I will keep on saying it, Make sure it's MADE IN AMERICA, BY AMERICANS AND AMERICAN-OWNED PLANTS. BE AMERICAN ... BUY AMERICAN.

Car Line	Country Built
Ford Crown Victoria	Canada
Ford Escort wagon	Mexico
Ford Esquire (same as Festiva)	Korea
Ford Probe	Joint venture with Mazda
Ford Windstar (new van)	Canada
Mercury Marquis	Canada

Mercury Tracer	Mexico
Mercury Villager minivan	Joint venture with Nissan
Chrysler Concord	All 1993s, Canada
	All 1994s, USA and Canada
Chrysler Intrepid	All 1993s, Canada
	All 1994s, USA and Canada
Chrysler New Yorker	All 1993s, Canada
	All 1994s, USA and Canada
Chrysler Eagle Vision	USA and Canada
Chrysler Dodge Shadow	USA and Mexico
Chrysler Dodge Spirit	USA and Mexico
Chrysler Eagle Summit	Japan
Chrysler Dodge Stealth	Japan
Chrysler Dodge van (all except the extended Caravan)	Canada
Chrysler Plymouth vans	Canada
Chrysler Plymouth Acclaim	Mexico
Chrysler Plymouth Duster	USA and Mexico
Chrysler Plymouth Sundance	USA and Mexico
Chrysler short-bed trucks	Mexico

All the above information came from Ford Motor Company World Headquarters Customer Assistance and the Chrysler Customer Assistance Center and various Ford, Lincoln Mercury, and Chrysler dealerships in the Detroit Metro area.

25

The End of the Beginning

by Rino Pagnucco

How do you write a conclusion about something that has not concluded yet? I mean, according to the dictionary, a conclusion means "an end." In this case, to me, it is the summation of this entire project. So, how do you write about something that hasn't ended yet, but if it continues the same way that it's been going, the end is sure to happen?

Americans and the American automobile industry have failed to realize that to the Japanese, "BUSINESS IS WAR." If you know anything about history, Japan sent many signals to America before they attacked Pearl Harbor, but no one would accept the fact that this little country would take on the greatest and most powerful country in the world.

We are at war again. We are in an economic war and a business war, and the strategy is the same: take away the present industry, put workers out of their jobs, and lessen the economy. Our once-strong power is not strong anymore. Have you ever heard the statement "the strong will survive"? You could bet your ass the Japanese have and, by the way, they now have the strongest economic base in the world. This war is not about bloodshed and bombs; it's about who's got the best plan, who's got the most patience, and, last but not least, who's got the most money.

It's also about loyalty. A U.S. marine or any other member of the armed services is so loyal to his country that he is willing to put his life on the line whenever needed. Well, this war is no different. I would bet you could not find a Chevy or a Ford or a Dodge or a Toyota in a parking lot where they build Hondas in Japan. Unless, of course, it was there for experimentation and research. I will never forget the large number of foreign cars, along with new Fords, in the salary parking lot of Pontiac Motor Division in Michigan during the time I worked there. By the way, that was as recent as 1991 and it is still going on. Most of these people have very good jobs in General Motors and EDS, but they always gave some excuse for not owning a GM vehicle, and the sad part here was that these excuses were accepted. They continued to get their raises and all the other benefits so they could help our competitors, who, in this economic war, are really the enemy. When this subject was brought up at the quarterly question-and-answer meetings, the divisional leaders just made more excuses. There is no acceptable excuse!

As Americans, we must realize that in order to win this war, we should only be buying American automobiles, owned by American companies, that are produced only here in America. Let me say this one more time. Built in America, by Americans, from an American automobile company. There are many American automobiles produced by General Motors, Ford, and Chrysler that are not made in America. These are the vehicles that we must be made knowledgeable of and "NOT" buy anymore. Hey, we're not just talking about this economic war; we're talking about jobs. Your job, my job, your children's future jobs. So, when you go into an American car dealership, ask them where the car was built. It's that easy. If it was built anywhere other than in the United States, DON'T BUY IT! Demand a comparable vehicle or, in some cases, the "same" vehicle that was built in the good old US of A.

What I'm trying to say is that we, as Americans, have been deceived. The commercial ad states "Here is the car that gave America rock-'n'-roll, the Chevrolet Camaro." Every one of these cars is built in Canada, along with every Pontiac Firebird. Buick is promoting "American quality," but every Buick Regal is built in Canada. How about the Chevy Tough Trucks? Most of them are built in Canada. The Ford Windstar, the Ford Crown Victoria, and the Mercury Marquis are all built in Canada. Chrysler's car lines the Intrepid, New Yorker, and Concord and almost every Chrysler van are made in Canada. But Chrysler is now graciously building some plants here in America to take care of the overflow that the Canadians can't handle. What's wrong with this picture? Shouldn't it be the other way around? No offense to our good neighbors to the north—I have many friends in Canada—and by no means any offense to any country that is building our cars and supplies, but it must "start" in America and when we can't keep up anymore, others can have the overflow.

So, buyer beware. Don't get hung up on that "bullshit" about those Hondas that are built here in Ohio and those Toyotas that are being built in Kentucky or those Mercedes-Benzs that are going to be built in Vance, Alabama, and those yuppie Beamers (BMWs) that are going to be built here in America. You'll hear that these companies have put us to work where our own companies have deserted us. This is the time to come to our senses and realize that the foreign car dollar first goes back to its original country and makes their economic base stronger so they have a better chance at winning this war. It's also the time to take that three-by-five card out of your pocket that says to the foreign car dealers: "GO FUCK YOURSELVES AND THE BOAT YOU CAME IN ON!"

I can't say this enough. The future of America and the future of the American automobile industry go hand in hand. Without the automotive industry, we virtually have no economy. The past has shown us that when the automobile industry is good, the economy is good. We buy cars; we build homes; we have low unemployment. We have more strength and security as a nation. Jobs, jobs, jobs, it's about jobs, jobs, jobs.

What I really mean when I say "we just do it to ourselves" is that the American automobile industry and Americans who buy foreign cars and cars that are not made in America are responsible for losing the economic war we are presently in. We cannot continue to close our plants and reopen newer and better plants in foreign countries. When we continue to open these plants in Canada, Asia, Europe, Russia, or wherever, we are committing manufacturing and economic suicide. Let me make it specifically clear here, I am not against helping other countries, but first we have to take care of our own. Let's make sure that everyone that has lost a job gets one back before we give one to someone else in another country. Let's make sure that when we shut down an old plant because of its old processes and its old way of thinking, we make sure that the hundreds of millions of dollars that we are spending on new factories in other countries be spent right here in our own country and on our own people first. Let "us" use the higher-tech equipment and let "us" build them smarter first. Give "us" the same chance that you are giving other countries. Let's face it, folks, the only thing we, the working people, both hourly and salary, did wrong . . . was follow orders. I mean, if we did so much wrong to the point of sending our jobs to another country, why did you allow us to continue? I don't understand, and now you want to give our jobs to another country, because they can follow orders better? I think what they are really trying to say is, "Let me try to get something straight between us!" The same management that is currently closing our plants in the United States is the same management that is going to run the new plants, which, in reality, is the same management that ran the old plants. I am really fucking confused. Let me remind you again that for every single automotive job that is lost, there are up to six nonrelated jobs in the community also affected in some way, if not also lost. When you close a factory down and put five thousand people out of work, another thirty thousand jobs are somehow affected. The clerk at Kmart isn't needed anymore, because of fewer sales, no one's buying, and you thought that small, menial job didn't mean anything. Well, it meant something to the person that was holding it, even if it was a part-time job for a high school student. Take these beginner starter jobs away from our youth and we take away the beginning.

This is where it starts. Now that the younger generation can't get a job, they also can't afford one of those GM cars. Even though we sent our jobs to another country, to take advantage of cheaper labor costs, we haven't lowered the price of the car. In fact, we continuously raise the price of the cars. Now, let's continue with this formula. We lay off the American workforce that once had the jobs, but we are not going to replace their jobs, so we have fewer, a lot fewer, jobs. Since we have fewer jobs, so we are now looking for jobs along with the new number of people without jobs, such as those high school and college graduates. There are fewer jobs and more people without jobs than ever before, and every year these numbers increase.

Now the General and the other American automobile companies can't sell the cars that they are now making in other countries to "those people," because they can't afford them either. Well, neither can the Americans, because they just lost their jobs. Is someone going to tell me that the Mexicans, for instance (it could be the Koreans or Russians or the people of any other country), that we are paying a very low wage per hour (somewhere between fifty-nine cents and three dollars an hour) are going to buy that $17,000 car?

So we don't sell as many cars as we used to, and the people at the top floors, no, at all the floors at that building on West Grand Boulevard, can't figure it out. Yet, these are the same people that put out the statement that said: "The majority of all the products that are sold by our corporation are sold to the people

192

that work for us." So if you keep getting rid of the people that work for you, guess what else you are getting rid of? If you guessed market share, you are not equal to the people running the business; you are "smarter" than them. You don't have to be a rocket scientist to figure this out.

So, while we are trying to figure out why we are our own worst enemy, the real enemy is watching and waiting. Little by little, they take another slice of the pie. They are very patient. They will never, ever, forget Pearl Harbor! They have also shown other countries how to get into the act. They have brought back the phrase "everybody is going to get rich." The people that say this are the people who are in "command," and it ain't us. The Japanese are very patient people. They always have a plan, and they are always willing to follow their plan. Remember, "PLAN YOUR WORK, WORK YOUR PLAN; FAIL TO PLAN, PLAN TO FAIL!" Time is on their side. They will bring in an automobile that is affordable. They will build it so well you won't want anything else. Don't forget, these people are very disciplined, crazy about detail, and are the best "copycats" in the world. So, the scenario here is: You just got laid off; you don't have a job. The job that you will get, if you get a job at all, will be a lower-paying job with a lot fewer benefits, if any at all. You not only lost your job, but also your loyalty. You still need a car to go to your new lower-paying job. Are you going to buy a car from the company that closed your plant and put it in another country? You now need a car that is dependable, quality-built, and affordable. You are now going to be treated with respect, you are going to be pampered, and now the price is going to be right. You, my friend, are hooked! The invasion of the economic and manufacturing war is on.

General Motors and America still believe, to this day, that Japan has to change when, in fact, the American people and the American automobile industry have to change. We not only have to become like them; we have to surpass them. America is the

193

most efficient country in the world, but Japan is the most efficient manufacturer in the world. They will also be, if they keep going in the direction they are going, especially with our help, the richest country in the world. Along with being the richest country in the world comes the status of being the most powerful country in the world. Just like the saying goes, "Money talks and bullshit walks!"

We are our own worst enemy? One of the best articles I have ever read was "Japan Attack on U.S.," by Scott LeBlanc on the Internet Bulletin Board, April 8, 1993. His article asked questions like: "Why do *we* have such a poor educational system in America? Why is *our* corporate management one of the worst in the world? Why, in the seventies, did America have the largest banks in the world and now nine out of ten of the largest banks in the world are owned by the Japanese?" It won't be long before Japan will be the only place that America is going to be able to borrow from. Between the poor jobs the politicians and corporate management have done with our budgets, we have dug ourselves a hole that we can't get out of without the financial help that only money can buy.

Ladies and gentlemen, boys and girls. Whether you are an Italian-American, Jewish-American, Polish-American, Irish-American, Spanish-American, Afro-American or whatever country you and your ancestors came from, if you live in and are a citizen of America, you are an AMERICAN. You should be proud and loyal to it. There are many residents of this great country getting benefits from our tax dollars that are "not" American citizens. If you are not proud enough to be an American citizen and continue to reap the benefits that we are handing out, please leave and go back to where you came from. We've got "real" Americans that we can share those tax dollars with, and for heaven's sake, quit your bitching. You may not agree with everything in America, but it's still, by far, the best country in

the world. Let all of us make it stronger than ever. BE AMERI-
CAN, BUY AMERICAN, and make sure it's MADE IN
AMERICA.

Rule #1

"If we don't take care of
our customers . . .
somebody else will.
—The Executive Gallery
Columbus, Ohio

SINCE 1990 GENERAL MOTORS
HAS LOST
OVER
$16.9 BILLION

A top GM executive in 1993 stated he was "pleased" that we
only lost $600 million in this quarter!